FROM GEEK TO LEAD

A TECHIE'S GUIDE TO LEADERSHIP

DR YOUSIF ASFOUR AND SANDY MOLLOY

info@geektolead.com
www.geektolead.com

Dr Yousif
Asfour

Yousif Asfour is an experienced technology executive with more than 20 years' experience as CIO and CTO in the USA and Middle East. He is a dynamic leader who has successfully built high performing teams and led the transformation of several organizations in various industries including technology, government, and higher education.

Yousif currently sits on the boards of several startups and serves as Chief Innovation and Transformation Officer at the American University of Beirut leading the Office of Information Technology, the Talal and Madiha Zein AUB Innovation Park, and the AUB Online Unit.

Most recently, Yousif was the President of the CIO Lebanon Association, the founding CIO at NYU Abu Dhabi, and played a key leadership role in establishing TechCARE, the Lebanese National Research and Education Network (NREN).

Yousif received a BS and MS in electrical engineering from Northeastern University and a PhD in cognitive and neural systems from Boston University. In addition to several publications in professional journals, Yousif also holds a patent related to fast data transfer for multiprocessor systems.

Sandy Molloy started her career in teaching at universities and colleges in Australia, Greece, USA, and the UK.

In the 90s she joined an American Global IT company and worked worldwide in Europe, Middle East and Africa in a variety of sectors. After some training in Organizational Development in the Learning Lab at MIT, she took on roles such as Director of People, Culture and Communications and Head of Leadership Development UK Operations and embedded processes for significant cultural change. She later consulted in team dynamics and leadership at New York University, Abu Dhabi and The American University of Beirut.

She is a NeuroLeadership coach and has written articles on leadership, managing change, and cultural transition. She studied leadership and lived with tribes in Kenya over an eleven year period and presented on television and radio.

Sandy has a passion and inexhaustible energy for helping people realize their full potential.

She is a Master of the Chartered Institute for Personnel Development, a psychometric practitioner and currently working on neuro somatic mindfulness.

Sandy
Molloy

i

FOREWORD

What an unexpected turn of events the second decade of this second millennium has brought for all of us in our own unique ways. We will, no doubt, continue to face rapid and often dramatic changes as we move into the future.

However, recent events have demonstrated that in difficult times, technologies and **Information Technology** (IT) have become even more invaluable and firmly embedded in our everyday lives.

The early 2020s pandemic required people to live, learn, and work differently, becoming more dependent on modern technologies. Technology has taken center stage.

For thousands of years, technology has been changing our lives, often dramatically. We have now reached an era of 'hyper change', where change is accelerating at an ever-increasing speed.

Embracing Change

People have always embraced new technologies to improve communication speed and efficiency. These globalization and technological advances have transformed tradi-tional businesses, industries, and education into a vision and economy based on information digitization.

Today, information technology users demand more innovative applications and quicker access to data. Consequently, we are seeing an increase in the workforce's engagement with information technology.

It is an exciting time for industries and businesses embracing and building on these technologies, providing IT professionals with exciting career opportunities that can take them from entry-level jobs to positions on the board, partnering for success.

These changes, however, will necessitate IT leaders becoming more business-focused and agile learners with a broader set of skills to meet the demands and needs of their stakeholders.

Information is abundant, and IT leaders must understand how to exploit the information and the technology to significantly transform their businesses and lives.

We are basing our suggestions in this book on years of experience in the IT environment, having both faced many challenges to update, change, shift the cultures and operating systems, and improve both the profile and perceptions of IT in the many environments we worked in.

We have used the activities and reading materials in the book to great effect and are eager to share them with professionals about to start their exciting leadership journeys. This book can also serve as an aide-mémoire for those already in leadership positions and looking for new ideas or who need to be reminded of things that may have slipped their minds over time.

Some of those journeys have been complex and challenging.

Still, the technical people we have met over our combined decades of working with IT organizations across the globe have an advantage in that they get enthusiastic about the technology. Generally referred to as techies, these professionals love a challenge. Leading them can also be a challenge.

In addition, organizations have higher expectations of their IT departments in terms of what can be delivered and when.

If IT departments are to be strategic business partners and add value to their organizations, then each IT professional in those

iii

BRIGHT
IDEAS

IT departments must play a vital role in helping the organization achieve its goals.

With more workers eager to learn new technology, the demand on those developing, implementing, operating, and supporting technology will require them to be flexible, willing, and able to upskill continuously.

In this book, we will introduce you to some of the key skills that we believe IT professionals should acquire, develop, and build on as they embark on their leadership journey.

IT and its transformative role in our lives is increasing and evolving rapidly.

IT is at the core of an era of 'hyper change', allowing organizations to adapt to ever-changing environments quickly.

We are heavily dependent on technology in every aspect of our lives. Consequently, we depend on the professionalism and skills of IT professionals.

Professionals joining the IT workforce are in greater demand today than ever before.

Businesses are expecting IT to transform them in meaningful ways.

IT professionals must continuously add new non-technical skills to their existing technical capabilities while keeping up with technological advances.

INTRODUCTION

We have both worked for decades in many IT environments across the globe and have concluded that some elements of leadership apply anywhere and everywhere in Information Technology and other businesses. **Leadership and its associated skills can be learned.** You can read many articles about what makes a good leader, but you may never reach all those 'ideals'. What you can do, however, is learn and improve your skills. It is a continuous journey because teams and contexts will change, and you need to be skillful at adapting and drawing on your previous experiences and lessons learned.

Being authentic and doing what you believe to be essential is more important than what you believe your job title requires of you.

It will take courage to make some changes to both your leadership style and the way you think. You may make mistakes, and that is fine.

Building relationships is a crucial life and leadership skill. As a leader, you will want to be trusted. You will want to have people connect and enjoy working with you. The ability to influence and persuade others is an essential skill in your leadership of IT teams and end users.

This book examines your work environment as an IT professional and how the IT landscape is changing. In this environment, you must adopt new ways of thinking to become a successful leader. Moreover, the demands placed on you will require new approaches to your work.

Our aim is to give you some guidance and help you, as new leaders, to manage better the technical professionals who will play an integral role in building the future success of their organizations.

We discuss the implications of a rapidly accelerating rate of change in a growing industry with demanding expectations, and we focus on how leaders can get better results faster.

Leading technical teams have their own set of requirements, and both technical and non-technical

'Space may not be the final frontier as we thought. Technology is a frontier on its own, continuing to evolve, grow and reshape our world. As we continue to explore and expand technology, the more life will change, creating new habits and forming new ways of working together.'
DISCOVER TEC

'Bad communication ends a lot of good things. Good communication ends a lot of bad things.'
FRANK VISCUSO

JARGON
ALERT!

GEN Z

Generation Z is a classification of people born between 1997 and 2013. As in previous generations, Gen Z are shaped by their sociopolitical and cultural environment. Rapid technological advances are a major influence on Gen Z entering employment and defining their careers. Leaders in organizations should be aware of the perceptions and attitudes of this growing workforce.

professionals will find that leading and managing techies can present its own set of challenges. We examine how technical and non-technical professionals approach work and get the best out of their leadership role.

We examine the issues that technical leaders are going to face. We will share our experiences as well as the experience of the technical teams that we have led and coached to help you meet the demands placed on leaders in IT today.

You will also encounter a new incoming workforce referred to as **Gen Z.** They have grown up with the Internet and have never known a life without technology. They have evolved into digital natives with

extensive skills in computer literacy and have different expectations from those around them, especially their leaders.

Gen Z professionals we have worked with recently profess to be more interested in authentic communication, focus differently on interpersonal and relationship skills, want flexible working arrangements, and expect more dialogue from the institutions that employ them. They expect to be able to challenge everyone they work with and for.

Building relationships is critical for any leader to progress, so we focus on ideas to help develop key communication skills and create trusting and open relationships.

The chapters on communication

and team building are extensive because, in our experience, these are two of the most pivotal areas of leadership.

These areas can have the biggest impact on how IT is perceived and how smoothly operations can run. Getting these skills early on can add value to the people leading, the people they lead, and the organization.

We offer actionable ideas and suggestions whether you are an IT professional thinking of becoming a leader or have been asked to lead technical teams.

These are presented in easily digestible pieces of information with examples drawn from real-life situations and from colleagues who have faced and addressed many leadership challenges. Each chapter includes ideas and templates to get you started.

We explain how, as IT professionals, you will need to fulfill the requirements expected of you. We help you to think about setting direction and achieving clarity in fast-paced environments. We also look at the areas in which we have seen leaders both grow and struggle with the leadership of technical teams.

Our focus is based explicitly on the management and leadership skills necessary to lead IT teams at the start of the leading process.

We know that leaders need other skills such as time management, project management, and the knowledge of other technical expertise and non-technical topics. We are also aware that how these skills are used is key to a leader's success.

However, our focus is primarily to help equip the first-time leader to transition from team member and individual contributor to a leader of technical people. These early days can make a big difference. We also look at the challenges facing the non-technical individuals leading a technical team. However, whether technical or non-technical, you will face the same issues of building and developing your teams, and we suggest several ways to get you started.

We sincerely hope you enjoy the read (even if you start from the back, as one of our techni-cal leaders did!) or dip in and out. We hope you can take away ideas and activities to get you started on the right path.

KEEP IN MIND

Throughout the book, we emphasize the importance and **power of asking the right questions.** We have learned over the years that this will help you avoid agreeing to unrealistic demands, avoid making the wrong assumptions, help you develop relationships, and deliver on managed expectations. We provide you with questions that you can use to assess yourself, your team members, the whole team, end users, and clients.

In the final section of the book and in a real case study that we both participated in, we demonstrated how the ideas we discussed were applied, how the outcomes were reached, and how they impacted the IT department and its stakeholders.

CONTENTS

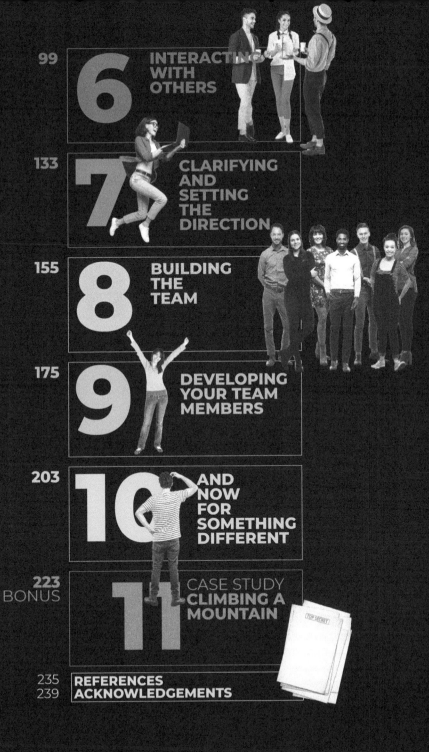

THE CHANGING ROLE OF INFORMATION TECHNOLOGY

In today's fast changing world, it's not what you know anymore that counts, because often what you know is old. It is how fast you learn. That skill is priceless.

ROBERT T KIYOSAKI

What is IT?

We use Information Technology (IT) as a general term that describes any technology that helps produce, manipulate, store, communicate, and /or disseminate information. This includes the development, implementation, and maintenance of computer hardware and software systems to organize and communicate information electronically.

The success of organizations today depends heavily on Information Technology.

Organizations would struggle to gain a competitive advantage or serve their customers and end users without their IT department partnering with the rest of the organizational units to drive innovation and transformation.

However, two significant environmental factors are changing how organizations view IT departments. To keep driving change, IT departments must transform themselves.

'Especially in technology, we need revolutionary change, not incremental change.'

LARRY
PAGE

The Challenge of IT Commoditization

The first of these environmental changes is the commoditization of technology.

The introduction of cloud services has created an environment where anyone can acquire and use cutting-edge technological tools to improve their work quickly and cheaply.

You can find financial, payroll, HR, and other Enterprise Resource Planning (ERP) tools online that are cheaper, easier

to use, and just as good as or better than the standard platforms used by businesses.

You can also find and implement databases, workflow engines, business intelligence, and process optimization tools, not to mention more sophisticated artificial intelligence and even factory tools, for a fraction of the cost and much faster than any IT department.

In most cases, you only need a credit card and no specialized technical knowledge.

While it is harder in some organizations than others, the fact is that it has become easier for anyone to buy and install anything by simply using their credit card, circumventing the IT departments This is partly due to IT being perceived as slow, bureaucratic, and irrelevant which creates a huge challenge for IT organizations. IT is responsible for ensuring data and system security through Confidentiality, Integrity, and Availability (or better yet, CIA).

When anyone can buy and use anything, we create 'islands of technology' and independent 'pools of data' that expose the organization to issues of:

ACRONYM
ALERT!

CONFIDENTIALITY
INTEGRITY
AVAILABILITY

Confidentiality
Privacy, governance, compliance.

Integrity
Duplication of data, stale data.

Availability
Ensuring the different fees are paid, licenses available, flow between different applications, access to the network.

In addition, end users view the ease of implementation and wealth of functionality

4

available with cloud services as the new standard and question why their IT department is so slow and expensive and sometimes fails to deliver.

The Anywhere Anytime Challenge

The second environmental change that has and continues to impact the transformation of IT is the COVID-19 pandemic.

The pandemic at the start of 2020 changed how and where people work. The need and desire for remote work and the creation of the virtual work environment created a new demand for IT groups and placed them at the core of the organization.

While this provided an opportunity for IT to shine, it also created new challenges, as IT has been universally expected to do no more than 'fix the computer'.

IT Must Become a Trusted Transformation Partner

So, what must IT departments do to play a key role in business transformation and become true transformation agents?

IT departments must first earn the trust of other departments by consistently providing exceptional service to the organization units. Once trust has been established, opportunities open up for IT to get involved in the design and implementation of the decision-making process, giving IT a leading role in transforming organizations.

This kind of change and transformation occurs when IT departments establish a baseline of the key services they provide, identifying what works

'What is sure is that technological change is accelerating in all directions, and like children playing in a fountain, consumers are reveling in the experience.'

SIMON MAINWARING

and the challenges and risks involved in making these changes.

Once a baseline has been established, the IT department can use it to improve service delivery and begin the transformation process.

But IT Must Transform Itself First

To achieve this, the IT organization must leverage cloud services to shift its focus from managing infrastructure to creating new value-added technology services that benefit the organization.

IT must also transform its role from a service provider that builds and operates technology services to a service broker who identifies third-party service providers and makes them accessible to the organization's end users.

This means that the IT department must also transform its staff from primarily engineers and technicians focused on technology to consultants and service managers capable of bridging the gap between technology and business.

Moreover, IT departments must move from 'builders' of services and systems to 'integrators' of service providers, technologies, and platforms.

But IT organizations must also transform their internal infrastructure from a 'castle and moat' model to a 'free-flowing city' model. That is, instead of depending on barriers to prevent the 'bad guys' from accessing the organizational infrastructure, IT needs to create an environment where folks can go anywhere 'safely'.

IT needs to create an infrastructure that allows anyone to connect from anywhere through any device at any time to any resource to do anything (which we call an 'Any' architecture) and move away from a 'Standards Enforcement' model to a 'if it fits, plug it in' model. In a nutshell, IT needs to transform.

IT Leaders Must Drive the Transformation

Information Technology team leaders must apply the appropriate leadership skills to navigate these challenges and exciting transformations.

IT leaders must define the mission and equip their teams with the needed skills, tools, and resources.

More importantly, IT leaders must be able to use their skills to create and drive change across multiple organizations within their enterprise while managing the repercussions that such changes produce.

Because of their involvement in all aspects of the organization, IT departments are uniquely positioned to know more than any other department about how the enterprise works.

Although Chief Information Officers and senior leadership in IT play an important role in this process, the key to success is consistent delivery and exhibiting the appropriate skills by the whole IT team. The leadership of, and within, these technical teams play a key role in making this happen.

Using the appropriate leadership skills from your first steps in IT up to the Chief Information Officer (CIO) role will help you handle challenges and get you a seat at the table where you can make fundamental changes to the organization's business.

This is the new world that the IT professional will need to adapt to.

ACRONYM ALERT!

CIO

CHIEF
INFORMATION
OFFICER

THE IT LEADER AS
PROCESS ENGINEER

In one of my previous CIO roles, the company's founder wanted to revamp all the processes to make the business more agile. He turned to the IT department for assistance.

'As the IT Leader,' he begins to explain his rationale to me, 'you are the only one in the organization who knows all the end-to-end processes and their interfaces across all organizational units.'

He pauses, and concludes with a straight face, 'So, you and your IT team are the most equipped to lead this effort.'

If IT is the eyes and ears of the organization, then IT leaders must communicate effectively to get the 'big picture' and capitalize on it.

—YA

The success of organizations today depends heavily on IT.

Anyone can circumvent the IT department.

IT is responsible for ensuring data and system security through CIA.

IT are uniquely positioned to know more than any other department about how the enterprise works.

IT must transform engineers into consultants to bridge the gap between technology and business.

This transformation must happen now.

OF
NERDS
AND
GEEKS

Then the whole town will gasp, 'Why this boy never sleeps! No keeper before ever kept what he keeps. There's no telling what that young fellow will do!' And then, just to show them, I'll sail to Katroo. And bring back an It-Kutch a Preep and a Proo, a Nerkle, a Nerd and a Seersucker too.

DR SEUSS

So Who Are These Technical Professionals?

First, let's answer a loaded question: Are IT professionals really that different?

Well, yes! Indeed, based on our experience. Of course, not fundamentally on a human level, but they can often live up to stereotypes attached to them.

Labeled as the 'geek', 'nerd', and the 'techie', these individuals have been the unseen mechanics behind the technical drivers of many businesses. Today, however, with a growing technical workforce and a rising need for information technology, these labels serve more of a compliment than an insult since their skills are in demand more than ever.

We appear to have shed the negative connotations of not belonging to the 'in-crowd'. After all, it is the 'geeks', 'nerds', and 'techies', like Nikola Tesla, Alan Turing, Bill Gates, Linus Torvalds, and Steve Wozniak, among others, who have shaped technologies with a global impact.

In What Ways Is a Technical Person Different?

Some IT professionals may have been inspired to use information technology at some critical point in their lives and subsequently found its real value.

Others, like young children who curiously pull apart an item to understand its mechanics, may have always been drawn to figuring out how things work.

Several technical professionals we spoke with about their passion for

technology said it began at a young age or during their adolescence.

Certainly, in today's world, young people are frequently competent users of, reliant on, and attracted to all the gadgets at their disposal, such as smaller laptops, tablets, smartphones, and smartwatches, just some of the technologies that make up the fabric of their lives.

Technical individuals can be perceived as earnest people who appear to be perpetually focused and preoccupied.

A Different Sense of Time

Do you find yourself taking work home and spending time thinking a problem through?

Many people have acknowledged losing their partners during what could be considered out-of-office hours.

The technical professional understands the importance of staying current with changing technological trends.

A team we spoke to said they always knew when their leader's wife was away because his emails with suggested ideas and possible solutions to existing problems kept coming in until late at night!

Have you ever noted the times of emails sent between technical people?

Also, some of you may have experience with roles that require out-of-office hours and VIP clients who call for assistance at any time.

Curiouser and Curiouser

Another characteristic of IT professionals is that they thrive on finding solutions to perceived problems.

Arc you curious, and can you immerse yourself in technical investigations? Do you enjoy engaging in technical conversations and problem-solving with peers and like-minded techie colleagues?

Leave Me Alone

Another characteristic often associated with technologists is their tendency to work alone, which may lead to the perception that they are loners. This perception is often misguided, as they may simply prefer to work independently on technology-related tasks. In fact, you can practically see their internal thought process as they tackle seemingly impossible tasks.

It's important to note that while technologists may exhibit introverted tendencies, this doesn't necessarily make them less effective communicators. However, some of them may often prefer to avoid taking the lead when it comes to communication.

'Introverts can be successful by recognizing and taking advantage of their strengths. For example, taking time for yourself to think and coming up with ideas.'

BILL GATES

INTROVERT

Carl Jung, a psychologist in the 1920s, developed the idea of personality types and their associated descriptions. His perspective on personality has been considered insightful for decades. He theorized that what appears to be random behavior results from differences in how people prefer to use their mental capacities. Jung also pointed out that we all have the capacity to develop the attributes of all types, but we also have preferences where we feel more comfortable. The term introvert usually refers to a personality type that prefers to think through issues on their own before discussing them with others and who needs time away from the noise of people to recharge.

They can work well both alone and in small groups. It's easy to see why the term is associated with technology.

Let Me Explain

On the other hand, some IT professionals with an engineering background will enjoy explaining in as much detail as possible how something works or why it does not.

As experts in their own field, information technology professionals enjoy trying to do the undoable.

Some of the technology professional's analytical skills may be innate, which is often why engineers choose this field. They then improve their abilities by learning new skills.

They can be resourceful in persisting through challenges and obstacles. We have also observed that they understand the importance of what they design, develop, integrate, and implement. This feeling of importance is gratifying, knowing their daily efforts are meaningful. Furthermore, they know that if the technology fails, it can lead to significant disruptions.

People are so reliant on information technology that they panic when something goes wrong. Part of the IT team's role is to reduce that stress.

IT professionals love analyzing and describing technological features. They fall back to discussing technical issues and have no objection to being labeled 'techies'. Over the course of years of training and development, we have heard them respond to some soft skills issues by stating that they are 'techies' and that, in some way, absolves them of the need to take a different approach!

Even senior leaders have been known to emphasize that their teams' techie brains function differently. It can be a challenge to help them value the softer skills, but many early issues in leadership are people-related rather than technical. Ignoring this fact can lead to costly mistakes in the beginning and make it more difficult to build trusting relationships.

Is That You?

OK, that was a description of the good features! Did you recognize any of those characteristics in yourself? What about the issues that are on the other side of the coin?

What Challenges Do These Differences Create?

So, in that account of the positive qualities, did you notice any of those traits in yourself? On the flip side, what about the negative aspects that accompany them?

The stereotype we discussed earlier depicts the nerd, geek, or techie as completely focused on the task at hand and who often enjoys working alone. While being focused is difficult to criticize, and some people may thrive on working alone, it can lead to an individual not feeling like they are a part of the team, not being perceived as a team player, and not engaging as a team player. This presents its own problems.

GEEK

Where does the word **geek** come from?

The word **geek** comes from the English and German words **geek and geck,** which mean **fool or freak.** The German word geck survives today and means fool. In 18th century Europe, **Gecken** were circus freaks.

In the 19th century, American **geeks** were still **circus freaks,** but they upped their game to include feats of freakishness, like biting the heads of live rats or chickens.

Modern geeks are not known for acts of barbarism (fortunately!) but still retain a flair for eccentricity. Today's **geek** is a person with **an intense interest in one or more subjects.** A geek will have an **encyclopedic knowledge** of these topics and may be an **avid collector** of related tech or memorabilia.

Geeks also tend **not to be fools** unless you consider their penchant for leading-edge technology foolish!

—SM

NERD

Where does the word **nerd** come from?

If you research the origin of the word **nerd**, you will find a fun but highly unlikely explanation that it was first used in the 1950 Dr Seuss story, 'If I Ran the Zoo,' in which a boy named Gerald McGrew made many delightfully extravagant claims about what he would do if he were in charge at the zoo.

While Dr Seuss may or may not have coined the term, there was a 1940s slang word, **nert,** which meant **crazy person.** Modern nerds could be considered **strange or fixated** because they are **preoccupied with topics of interest.** These are typically academic pursuits but have also been associated with technology or gadget fans.

A more modern definition is that a nerd is an **intellectual intent on fully comprehending** one or more topics while **mastering the skills of the discipline.**

Some would say a nerd is a **geek who lacks social skills** or prefers solitary pursuits.

Interestingly the Urban Dictionary throws up a definition that may bring a smile to your face and defines nerds as **'a four-letter word with a six-figure income.'**

—SM

Hocus Focus

Being highly focused can sometimes result in being fixated and determined to find a solution at all costs, leading to excessive time resolving an issue. In our experience, time management is frequently (if not always) a problem. Technology for the sake of technology is no longer sufficient. Does any of this sound familiar to you yet?

In certain sections of the IT department, there have been instances where individuals have become overly attached to their projects and worked in isolation. However, this approach is not effective when end users and clients require solutions to their problems rather than the mere creation of a product. Most end users are interested in what works rather than how it is developed.

There is no I in Team

Organizations today, more than ever, require effective teamwork and solid business expertise to achieve their goals. Working alone may cause delays, and the field of information technology is moving much faster. Furthermore, people expect things to be resolved and delivered quickly.

As a technology professional, have you read hefty manuals? Written them? Have you developed and built structures or traced and designed processes? Do you have a strong desire to implement the solution in a process? You may be nodding to yourself now.

Leadership Readership

Unfortunately, in our experience, despite enthusiastically reading technical materials, most IT professionals we have worked with were not particularly enthusiastic about reading leadership or self-development books outside of their technical arena. They prefer quick tips and advice.

When you start to lead, you will soon appreciate the value of the available resources around you. We hope this book will become one of your helpful resources.

Technical professionals tend only to respect experts in their field and are eager to learn from the 'best'— those with technical and operational expertise.

Therefore, you must, at a minimum, understand their language and relate to their challenges when training and developing their leadership skills.

In the next chapter, we look at the technical and non-technical challenges of leading technical teams.

'My younger grandchildren manage to teach me something new about the technology they and I use each time I see them!'

SANDY MOLLOY

A WORD OF CAUTION

We may not necessarily know the psychology behind people's behavior or need to accept or learn any definitive theories, but we do **need to develop the skill of relating to the people we work with,** who behave differently from ourselves. **When leading people, it is essential to recognize these differences.** Engage them to maximize their potential and help them develop in challenging areas. However, **we need to be wary of labeling people!** Even if they themselves use such terms.

Believe it! Technical people are different, and leading their team is a unique experience with its own challenges and rewards.

IT professionals present two sides of the same coin: they may see the tree and not notice the forest.

And yet, they may describe the ecosystem of the entire forest when you only ask about one single plant!

We need to move away from the stereotype of IT professionals and toward a new perspective that recognizes their contribution to creating and building our ever-changing environment.

The IT professionals will have a major part to play in the required shift of mindset.

Future demands will necessitate the development of communication and information-sharing abilities.

IT will need to be the I of information as well as the T of technology.

The quality of the communication and information systems is critical.

Some technology professionals lack well-developed softer skills, but today businesses demand more effective communication skills.

Their knowledge and ability to communicate that knowledge and build long-term relationships will be crucial to their personal and organizational success in the future.

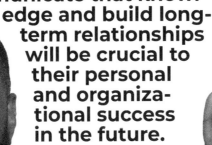

LEADING
THE
TEAM

Technology by itself doesn't make leaders. Technology only amplifies true leadership.

STEVE JOBS

So, You're Taking on a Leadership Role

Several circumstances may result in you taking on a leadership role. You may have chosen this as part of your career path.

You may be asked to lead because of attrition, ie, when a leader leaves the team or the department. This could be because nobody else has applied for the job, or you were seen as the best person for the role. You could also be asked to lead for an interim period or permanently if recognized as having the potential to be a great leader.

Whatever brings you into the role, you need to ask yourself a few questions about how you operate, what your teams will expect from you, where to focus your attention, and which behaviors you should be more conscious of.

Working with technical teams can be challenging. You have to define the scope of the work, determine a technical approach, estimate timelines, deal with the complexities of end users and business expectations, and get people to work together.

Making the Move

If you are moving from a technical team member to a leader or joining as a non-technical leader, your responsibilities will extend beyond technical skills. As an IT leader, your team may appreciate your technical knowledge and expertise, but just as with leading non-technical teams, you will also be expected to solve problems, create visions, and ensure that everyone understands their roles and what is expected of them.

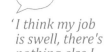

'*I think my job is swell, there's nothing else I love so well.*

I love to work among my peers, I love their leers, and jeers, and sneers.

I love my computer and its software; I hug it often though it won't care.'

DR SEUSS

It's also important to understand your team's expertise and how they fit into the larger IT organization. Finally, you must establish effective communication channels to build trust and confidence in your decisions.

You will also become more of a 'go-to person' for your stakeholders and other departments within the organization (in and outside of the team). You must keep track of what everyone is working on, delegate tasks, and give your team members ownership of issues while remaining accountable for their resolution. Finally, match your team's skills and resources to the required outcomes.

Technicalities for Technical Leadership

As a technical team member, we strongly encourage you to develop specific leadership skills in addition to technical expertise.

This may or may not differentiate a technical team leader from new leaders in other areas of an organization, but the engineering brain is more focused on technical complexities and less on people skills. Often, they begin this journey still focused on the technological aspects of their jobs. Similarly, some leading others for the first time may know what to do theoretically but need to learn how to do it.

Although there may be some differences between a technical expert and a non-technical person assuming leadership, certain fundamental principles apply to both.

Managing a technical team can be especially difficult because the leader's expertise must earn the respect of the team members, especially if it is in their own area of technology. This means that a non-technical manager may face even greater difficulties in gaining the trust and respect of his team members.

But Don't Worry if You're Not a Techie

Business leaders often progress in their leadership careers for reasons not necessarily reflected in their curriculum vitae.

If you are a leader from a non-technical background, the team must feel confident that you have acceptable expertise in technology and that you will make sound technical decisions based on the information you gather from the team and other experts you may consult.

To begin building this confidence, you must explain clearly to the team what your goals are. As a non-technical leader, you must understand what your team is working on, what part of the system or business process they are managing, and how they make decisions.

Many leaders do this by conducting daily check-ins with the team, remotely or in person, and including the entire team.

If people are hesitant to participate in the discussion, then keep the meetings brief and focused on top priorities rather than allowing them to escalate into problem-

THANK GOODNESS I'M NOT A TECHIE!

When we asked Claire how she felt leading people with more technical knowledge, she said, 'thank goodness for that! That's what I say.'

She told us that she felt confident in her abilities and knew she could set sail, plot a course, use the rudder, and polish and clean up the boat.

But she was adamant that she would always need people to use the radar and sonar, see the obstacles in the way and know how the engine worked.

—SM

solving sessions. These can be dealt with outside of meetings.

You must work out what makes the technical people tick. Spend time with members of the team (we will be giving you ideas on how to do this later) and start learning from them by piecing together the work.

Understanding how other parts of the IT organization work is beneficial because you'll interact with them more than you have in the past.

The non-technical leaders we have worked with suggested that, as a minimum, they needed to gain some domain knowledge from their team members and were constantly learning.

ON SELECTING A CIO

On joining an organization, the newly appointed CIO discovered that he was the 'second choice', and that he got selected only because the first choice rejected the offer.

Although both CIOs were equally technical, the 'first choice' CIO spent most of the time during the selection process with the IT team in the data center, asking about the specifications of the equipment and system configuration.

The 'second choice' CIO spent most of the time talking and

Engage with Your Team

It is useful to have regular forums with the team where they are given the opportunity to have technical debriefs. You may not necessarily have the team's expertise. However, you can still help facilitate the conversation, listen, and manage the group discussion to ensure everyone can voice their concerns and maintain a balanced conversation.

Increasing your knowledge in the subject matter will also enable you, as the leader, to ask insightful and thought-provoking questions that challenge the team and earn their respect.

asking about people and organizational issues to understand better the culture and how best to lead.

The selection committee depended heavily on the feedback from the IT team, who could only see value from a 'technical perspective', and recommended the 'technical CIO'.

It turns out that the 'second choice' appointed to the role ended up being the 'better choice'. Not only did he possess technical expertise, but he was also able to address many team and relationship issues that his predecessor failed to address.

Several months into his new job, the 'second choice' CIO was approached by one of the team members: 'We didn't think you were technical, so we didn't pick you. But I'm glad you made it here, the 'technical CIO' wouldn't have been able to fix our problems'.

Although technical skills are important, having skills to deal effectively with people is critical at every level of leadership. Organizations have yet to recognize this.

—YA

BUILD YOUR NETWORK TO BUILD KNOWLEDGE

John told us that he thought his lack of technical knowledge in some areas was offset by building a network of people with strong IT skills.

This helped him build up his knowledge of the environment, and he relied on domain experts for specifics.

He learned more about the domains and was able to use this knowledge to ask his team the right questions.

The team trusted him because he challenged them with thought-provoking questions.

He helped them expand their networks and connected them with various specialists.

—SM

For cxample, one leader we spoke with suggested several things that had worked for her in the early days: ask them to draw a real-time diagram in front of you with a pen and paper to explain the work, change, or issue at hand.

Technical people enjoy drawing diagrams and figuring out how to explain them.

Ask Them to Engage

Inquire about any potential interface issues, integration with other necessary systems or networks, or anything relevant to the subject.

Ask them how they can prove it (ie, how do they know?). If you feel a team member is taking advantage of your lack of technical know-how, suggest a peer review with other team members who are equally, if not more, knowledgeable.

You could also ask someone to join a conference call or visit the team in person. Inquire if other team members share the same opinion or have reached the same conclusion.

Additionally, you can ask how and with whom they validated any assumptions, issues, risks, or constraints. These may sound like more project-related questions, but they work just as well with technical challenges.

You could also inquire about the versions being used and ask whether they would be doing things differently if they had more funding, time, or team members.

Encourage peer reviews (formal or informal) as the norm to ensure accuracy and challenge assumptions.

Make It Safe to Share

Help your team understand that you will ask questions as the team leader. In this way, you can also teach the team that it is okay to be wrong and, more importantly, to be honest and transparent. Asking questions will increase your knowledge and create a culture of accountability.

It would be a bigger problem if technical team members used their technical knowledge to avoid doing something or to explain away an issue. So check the information you receive with others, and be prepared to ask probing questions to get a bigger picture. This will assist you in avoiding a difficult situation if a team member takes advantage of your lack of technical expertise or is lazy or duplicitous.

You can also gain domain knowledge by researching and networking with supportive peers outside the organization. It is an excellent way to understand how certain technical areas work, their features, applications, challenges, and benefits so that you can ask the appropriate questions at the right time.

'Becoming a leader is synonymous with becoming yourself. It is precisely that simple and its also that difficult.'

WARREN BENNIS

Act As a Conduit

If you are not a domain expert and cannot solve the problem, it is more effective to act as a conduit.

But do not fake it. Faking it will earn you little trust or respect from the team, making management more difficult (as it would in any team).

On the plus side, as a non-expert leader, you may have an advantage over the technical leader because you cannot solve the technical problem personally. Some technical IT leaders struggle with delegating technical tasks and often find it difficult to let go of doing the technical fixes themselves. As time constraints are often an issue they may fail to coach their team to do it themselves.

A senior leader recently told us that promoting a valuable technical person to a leadership role had caused numerous problems in the team because he could not resist doing things himself, leaving the team feeling undermined. It changed the dynamic of a previously productive team.

Technical people may be accustomed to doing things their way, but this may not always be acceptable to others on their team when you start to lead them.

Non-technical people must build on the different approaches of the team until they find the most effective ways to achieve their goals.

To some extent, those early days of leadership will be a steep learning curve and may feel primarily administrative, but the necessary leadership skills can be learned on the job.

You do not have to rush into this. Instead, take time to assess what you need to know and how you will do it. In later chapters, we will look into some of those skills and suggest ways to get the team to work with you.

Remember that some of these abilities are not dependent on your technical knowledge.

Get To Know the People You Serve

Take the time to learn about your end users and stakeholders and what they expect from your team.

Make sure you and your team clearly understand the goals you want to achieve and how your work is interdependent with the rest of your organization.

Get to know the team and think about how you can help them overcome some obstacles. Make yourself available to assist them with their problems.

GAIN RESPECT BY DEVELOPING YOUR PEOPLE

Josephine had technical expertise in one area of IT but had to lead a technical team whose expertise was outside her experience. She noted that her team was gaining respect for her when they realized she was engaged in people management as well as setting clear objectives, identifying clear processes, and managing performance issues.

She also supported their career growth by helping them develop the necessary skills to succeed as individuals and as a team. She learned a lot from the team due to these types of communication.

She also worked hard to understand other areas of IT by collaborating with subject matter experts.

—SM

Understand what they expect of their leader and be clear about what you want from them. These discussions rely on something other than your technical knowledge in their areas of expertise in the IT organization.

You will face some difficulties, but the technical specialist who takes on the team leader role in an IT department will also face some challenges.

Learn to Let Go

If an organization is developing its people from within and has a solid knowledge of the business and its members, it is common for technical team members to transition into leadership roles within their team.

This does not guarantee success as a leader; the best technical individual does not always make the best technical team leader.

Although technical skills may have been recognized, there also needs

TO DO OR NOT TO DO.

David found his new role as a technical team leader very difficult. He had enjoyed his technical role and found himself drawn to the 'nuts and bolts' of things. As a result, his team felt micromanaged and distrusted. One of his team members found it difficult to accept him as the new leader while he continued to do the same things he had done as a team member. David began to sense that the team had become uncomfortable, and he realized that he could not manage all of the team's activities while also attempting technical work. He had reached a point in his career where he needed to be less hands-on technically and concentrate on the other aspects of technical leadership. He admitted it had been a tough transition to **let go,** but essential.

—SM

to be some preparation for leadership. This does happen in some organizations but needs to be factored into a team's development and succession planning. Sadly, this is not always the case.

Regardless of whether this level of preparation exists, when a new leader is promoted from within, both the team and the newly appointed leader must make many adjustments.

You may have done things a certain way and enjoyed good relations with your previous leader, but you could have had issues with how other team members worked.

But now, as their leader, it is part of your job to help these people develop and grow and not necessarily do things as you have done in the past.

You have the opportunity to coach, advise, and learn from your team members.

As a technical manager, you must consider when to give your input, when and how to make decisions that impact people, and when to delegate authority to the team based on their skills and abilities.

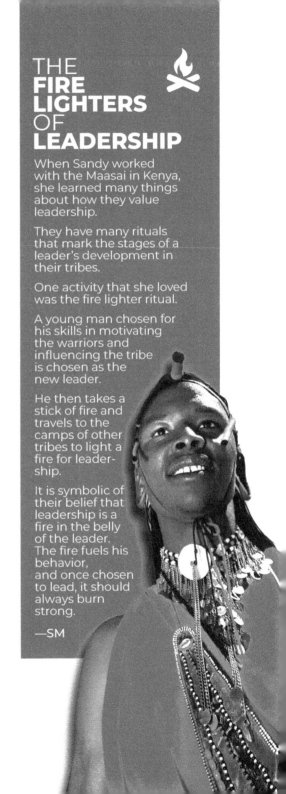

THE FIRE LIGHTERS OF LEADERSHIP

When Sandy worked with the Maasai in Kenya, she learned many things about how they value leadership.

They have many rituals that mark the stages of a leader's development in their tribes.

One activity that she loved was the fire lighter ritual.

A young man chosen for his skills in motivating the warriors and influencing the tribe is chosen as the new leader.

He then takes a stick of fire and travels to the camps of other tribes to light a fire for leadership.

It is symbolic of their belief that leadership is a fire in the belly of the leader. The fire fuels his behavior, and once chosen to lead, it should always burn strong.

—SM

The most important lesson you must learn is to 'let go'. Your role will change, as will your relationship with your team members, and you will be expected to be a role model for what you say and do in the future.

Stay Up to Date

As a leader with a technical background, you will have the advantage of understanding the technology your team uses and will be expected to use, but it's important to keep up to date too. Furthermore, as you communicate with a broader range of people and expand your professional network, you must translate your technical knowledge into more refined communications skills.

Define What Needs to Be Done

When considering a leadership role, whether technical or non-technical, you should consider three factors:

Knowing what you want and will need to do.

Knowing how to do it.

Creating opportunities to do it.

If you are pursuing a career in leadership, you may have already thought about what you want to do and what you'll need to do when leading a team, but it's also important to know HOW to develop the skills you need to be an effective leader.

You will almost certainly need to invest more time, use more energy, and require more self-management (and self-awareness) and vitality than you initially imagined.

Build and Nurture Relationships

In our experience, leaders of technical teams become successful when they put their efforts into developing relationships with their teams and genuinely care about what they do, what they can learn, and how they can help their teams succeed.

Participants in training sessions are often asked, 'What makes a great leader?' The answers are limitless and vary according to the situation.

Many skills may seem unattainable at the start of a leader's career. Nobody is perfect. In the next few chapters, we offer some ideas, based on our experiences, of a few essential basic things that will get you started on your leadership journey.

Some basics remain constant regardless of the environment; you must adapt them to suit you, your followers, and your organization.

LEADERSHIP

- ☐ Am I aware of my strengths, and do I know how to add value to them?

- ☐ How will I use each strength to build trust with the team?

- ☐ What triggers me, and do I have beliefs about how work should be completed and how I prefer to work? (Not everyone will work in the same manner as you, so understanding their style of work and supporting or improving those is essential).

- ☐ Am I aware of the accountabilities I will now have as a leader?

- ☐ Do I have plans for balancing people management, building processes, and managing performance?

- ☐ What will I need to do to provide feedback to team members who were previously my peers?

- ☐ Am I comfortable asking for feedback to keep assumptions from replacing facts?

- ☐ How will I manage relationships with people I consider friends?

- ☐ How can I change people's perceptions of me from a friend to a leader?

WORKSHEET 3.1

In the meantime, consider the following questions as you prepare for a leadership role. Keep this template nearby so you can refer to it at the end of the book and after a few weeks in the position to see what you have learned and how your ideas have shifted or been reaffirmed.

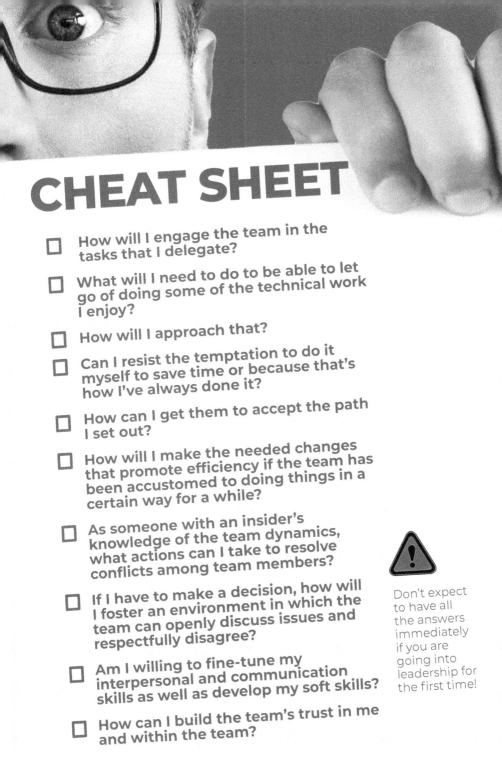

CHEAT SHEET

- [ ] How will I engage the team in the tasks that I delegate?

- [ ] What will I need to do to be able to let go of doing some of the technical work I enjoy?

- [ ] How will I approach that?

- [ ] Can I resist the temptation to do it myself to save time or because that's how I've always done it?

- [ ] How can I get them to accept the path I set out?

- [ ] How will I make the needed changes that promote efficiency if the team has been accustomed to doing things in a certain way for a while?

- [ ] As someone with an insider's knowledge of the team dynamics, what actions can I take to resolve conflicts among team members?

- [ ] If I have to make a decision, how will I foster an environment in which the team can openly discuss issues and respectfully disagree?

- [ ] Am I willing to fine-tune my interpersonal and communication skills as well as develop my soft skills?

- [ ] How can I build the team's trust in me and within the team?

Don't expect to have all the answers immediately if you are going into leadership for the first time!

It's a Continuous Learning Process

Leadership, fortunately, can be learned and is an ongoing process. It is nearly impossible to master everything, which is why many senior executives work with coaches and mentors.

In the next chapter, we start the process by focusing on **you**. By increasing your self-awareness, you begin to equip yourself for a leadership role better. This has little to do with your technical expertise, so the technical and non-technical leader is on the same start line to a certain extent.

Technical teams expect and respect a leader with technical knowledge.

Whether technical or non-technical, the leader must strongly desire to learn and stay current on technological trends.

Take time to learn the fundamentals and rely on team members and outside experts for assistance.

You may need to emphasize fundamental concepts with your questions.

Doing so will help the team communicate clearly and allow you to learn from them as you go.

Be prepared to examine your ideas and beliefs about leadership.

Take some time to consider your role in the new leadership position.

KNOWING
YOURSELF

Be yourself-more-with skill.

ROB GOFFEE
AND GARETH JONES

It All Starts With YOU

So, before you take on the leadership role, where do you start?

It may feel exciting, daunting, or challenging, or you may feel you know enough about the team and the role and just want to get going.

But where do you start?

We suggest the best place to start is with **YOU**. Take time to reflect on and consider some aspects of yourself now that you are becoming a leader.

You may have invested much time and energy in developing your technical skills and competencies and may have been recognized for your performance. But the workplace rules are changing, and you will no longer be assessed solely on your technical skills. When you assume a leadership role, you will be evaluated on other skills, with greater emphasis on how you handle yourself and others. Numerous books outline the characteristics of great leaders. Do not imitate them. Just be yourself but with greater skills.

You will need to expand your knowledge, recognize your limitations while remaining confident, create your own tool kit, and develop that extra something that leadership requires.

'Leaders are what makes up the spirit of the organization.'

PETER SENGE

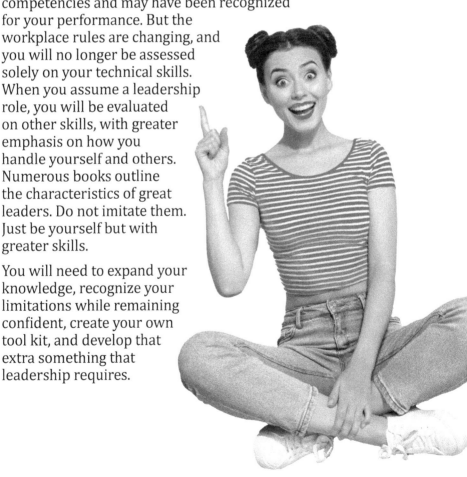

Organizations require managers to operate and develop well-thought-out systems and performance metrics. However, they also need leaders who can connect, relate, and engage with others, strive for great outcomes, and help their organizations succeed.

In today's evolving business landscapes, effective leaders must act as both 'guides and travelers', reflecting the diverse geography and the makeup of their organization. As their guide and traveler, you will bring that 'something extra' to your team!

THE SOUND OF SILENCE

When Miikka's wife gets upset with the children, nothing happens.
However, when he is upset with them, the whole household goes silent.

The difference: His wife gets emotional, and he stays calm. She lets them know she is mad, and he lets them know he is disappointed. He is quiet, and she is loud.

The same applies at work.

—YA

Be Authentic

In recent conversations with people we coach, we have noted that younger leaders frequently use the word authenticity. It has gained importance in this new generation of professionals and has become part of their everyday vocabulary. It is what they expect of their leaders.

In their book, *Why Should Anyone Be Led by You?* Rob Goffee and Gareth Jones suggest that being authentic is a great attribute of successful leadership. (We have already mentioned that faking it with your team, technical or otherwise, is useless).

They assert that some qualities, such as exposing vulnerability (showing you are human), showing tough empathy (giving people what they need, not necessarily what they want), being passionate and realistic, and capitalizing on your own unique strengths, will motivate people to follow you.

'*Authenticity is the alignment of head, mouth, heart, and feet—thinking, saying, feeling, and doing the same thing— consistently.'*

LANCE SECRETAN

Never Stop Learning

Goffee and Jones suggest that '*being yourself, in context, with skill*' will help you become a more successful authentic leader.

It is also important to recognize that leadership will be an ongoing learning process. We have both worked with experienced CEOs of companies still learning and looking to expand their skills.

But it's not just *learning* for the sake of learning but also *learning from* your experiences and the people around you. This can also assist you in developing a mindset that views failures as learning opportunities for continuous improvement.

So, if the key is to be *yourself* more skillfully, you will need to get to know *yourself* better.

Try to be aware of how you react to different situations and what others say. This will help you improve yourself and focus on changing your relationships and interactions with others.

Manage Your Emotions

Your authentic self will become even more important as you become more self-aware. Learning to control your actions and behaviors will highly benefit your continuous personal growth.

Daniel Goleman, although not the founder of the research on emotional intelligence, popularized the concept with his framework of key components that make up emotional intelligence.

He suggests starting with your emotional response, self-management, and self-motivation to develop emotional intelligence.

Once you start working on this area of personal growth, you can begin to understand other people's actions and how your behavior affects them. Social awareness helps you manage the relationships and emotions of others.

It is difficult to gain respect or trust from those you lead if you cannot control your emotions while criticizing their abilities and behaviors.

Goleman's framework comprises four quadrants, often referred to as the Four Pillars.

Organizations are increasingly aware of the importance of emotional intelligence in helping leaders drive their businesses forward with engaged and productive teams.

The new generation of employees joining the workforce can also relate to this.

'Emotional intelligence is the ability to understand and manage your own emotions and feelings, as well as those of others.'

DANIEL
GOLEMAN

	RECOGNITION	**REGULATION**
PERSONAL COMPETENCE	**SELF** AWARENESS SELF CONFIDENCE EMOTIONAL AWARENESS IMPACT ON OTHERS OTHERS' INFLUENCE	**SELF** MANAGEMENT CHECKING EMOTIONS AND IMPULSES MAINTAINING VALUES HANDLING CHANGE FOCUSING ON OPPORTUNITIES
SOCIAL COMPETENCE 	**SOCIAL** AWARENESS ROOM MOOD AWARENESS EMPATHY WITH OTHERS ACTIVE LISTENING	**SOCIAL** MANAGEMENT GETTING ALONG WITH OTHERS HANDLING CONFLICT CLEARLY COMMUNICATING USING EMPATHY TO MANAGE INTERACTIONS

An emotionally intelligent leader can help motivate the team, make them feel more included, and reflect a communication style that fosters a more productive culture.

FIGURE 4.1
THE FOUR PILLARS OF EMOTIONAL INTELLIGENCE
DANIEL GOLEMAN

However, developing emotional intelligence is not about getting high scores. You may be more competent in some areas and weaker in others.

This book encourages you to continue learning and growing in all areas.

People are complex, and it takes time and effort to know ourselves better and develop empathy to understand and manage others.

So, let's look at seven ideas to get you going.

1 Solicit and Act on Feedback

If what you need to do is be authentic, then the **how** is to start developing your self-awareness.

Emotional intelligence is a challenging task to master on your own. You may understand the concepts but ask yourself so now what?

First, solicit feedback. Then work on the areas that other people have identified. Seek people willing to offer you feedback on your behavior with the intention of helping you improve. Be willing to act on their suggestions.

We have coached leaders who disagreed with their peers, team members, or leader. But by supporting them, they were able to gain their own insights into how their behavior and interactions affect others. They were then able to make small yet impactful behavioral changes.

Once you start to make these changes and become more conscious of your behavior, you

will discover new areas to focus on and improve. Seeing the positive effects of these changes on yourself and others encourages you to continue improving. Read the case study of Rabih in chapter 5. It is a powerful message.

Follow up with the people who gave you feedback to see if they have noticed any changes. We all have blind spots regarding our behavior and have certain beliefs and experiences that can shape how we think and act. Getting a reality check from others can help you recognize these areas and see how you are perceived.

In some organizations, there are assessments to help leaders develop these skills. If this is not available to you, several tools in the market can encourage you to reflect on and develop your leadership abilities.

Take your time looking at things without passing judgment on yourself.

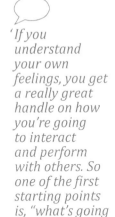

'If you understand your own feelings, you get a really great handle on how you're going to interact and perform with others. So one of the first starting points is, "what's going on inside of me?"'

CHUCK WOLFE

2 Reflect On Your Actions

Reflecting on our actions allows us to learn valuable lessons. By analyzing our behavior and its impact, we can avoid blaming others or feeling like a victim.

Taking responsibility for our behavior and working to improve it can be rewarding.

One of the leaders we worked with informed us that her immediate team leader believed she lacked spontaneity and that the rigid structure harmed relationships.

After becoming self-aware, the leader found that by focusing on one area, she could gain insight into other aspects of her behavior and use this to help her achieve her leadership goals. She began taking small actions every day. Her colleagues soon noticed her efforts, increasing team morale.

We work with all types of people and situations every day, and it is helpful always to consider your emotional response to the actions of others.

3 Slow Things Down

Adopt an SPR approach. When **S**omething occurs, **P**ause and **P**rocess what is going on and then **R**espond appropriately to the situation.

The gap between the stimulus (S) and the response (R) is the gap where you can make choices and decisions (P).

ACRONYM ALERT!

SPR

SOMETHING OCCURS

PAUSE AND PROCESS

RESPOND APPROPRIATELY

Another way you can deal with your emotional responses might be to simply say,

'Thank you for letting me know.'

'Give me a minute to think about that.'

'I'll think about it, and I'll get back to you tomorrow.'

Slowing things down may feel like a long time to you, but in terms of getting a more productive outcome, it's no time at all. The more you do this, the more people will expect you to give thought to things and not simply react.

Share your thoughts with a trusted colleague, friend, or leader to get useful feedback and positive reinforcement when appropriate.

Take time to think 'SPR' before you go into a contentious meeting or you are in a situation where you can sense negativity in yourself.

Simply saying it to your brain can relieve tension and buy you time to regain control.

When you take time to reflect on the things you do and say, you can make changes and adjustments.

John was very upset because a couple of his colleagues were fired that morning after being accused of a serious breach of protocol.

John took this very personally because he contributed to the information that led to their firing and believed what was done was completely unfair.

He blamed senior managers for making an unfair decision and felt he was the victim of a setup by his boss.

As unfair as it seemed to John, the decision by his leaders to fire his colleagues had been well thought out and based on information that John did not have access to.

As a leader on the team, John was expected to trust his leadership and work with them to smooth out the ramifications of the decision with the team instead of becoming part of the problem.

Instead, John felt very aggrieved.

—SM

WORKSHEET 4.1
As a leader in John's shoes, how would you have applied SPR—and managed your emotions—to handle the situation better?

1
2
3

4 Write Things Down

Another useful tool to add to your tool kit is to jot things down so that you can look back at your reactions and thoughts. The distance may help you see things in a different light.

Also, when writing down talking points, you get the chance to be clearer about what you want to articulate and allow yourself to remove the emotions from what you need to say.

This also applies to writing emails when you feel emotional. We spoke to the leaders of first time leaders, who told us they often had to spend time smoothing things out when these new leaders flexed their muscles in emails.

Write it if it makes you feel better but keep it as a draft. When you have calmed down, you will have control over your choices. When you read it, consider how the reader might understand it and clarify the meaning.

ON BEING MORE OPEN

Ross believed you should keep your weaknesses private from your leaders because they hired you to do the best job possible.

When Ross spoke to his boss, he always maintained that everything was good and thoroughly detailed everything he did to be seen as professional.

Ross's boss, however, was hearing feedback from the team, and felt that Ross showed no genuine warmth. He was uncomfortable with his decision to put him in a leadership position. Ross's team also felt that they could

not give Ross bad news or the full picture. This also revealed that Ross had to work much harder than necessary to avoid telling his boss about problems.

When Ross and his boss discussed this, his boss re- emphasized that he was there to help Ross become more self-aware and provide help and

guidance where necessary.

Ross worked on his behavior and began questioning his belief that you don't discuss failures or ask for help.

It would mean a change in behavior for him,

but he realized that focusing on what made others uncomfortable was not at odds with his being authentic. He also acknowledged that he did make mistakes, as did others, but he could ask for help.

His relationships improved, and Ross tried hard to acquire techniques that helped him better relate to people. He also told his team what he was working on. This resulted in a better understanding from his team, and Ross was able to let them freely discuss their problem areas so that he could help them learn.

—SM

TWO WAYS TO
HAVE THE SAME
CONVERSATION

1a Hey Byron, my team is not getting any support from your team at all!

AE-CHA

2b Byron pauses and thinks about the response. He is using the ability to choose how to respond without just reacting to something that has created an emotional response.

I don't think that's true, Ae-Cha! They are all working very hard to get things completed.

BYRON

2a

3b OK, Ae-Cha, that's not good to hear. What do you feel is happening?

Well, it doesn't look like that, and my team is getting very frustrated and fed up.

3a

4b Where do you think the problems are? Which areas or people are affected or feel unsupported?

5b

What are the facts? I gotta leave my emotions out of this. What actions should I take to change the perception?

4a

6b

DON'T

5a And the conversation rattles on, getting emotional and defensive.

7b In this approach, Byron manages his emotions, and in regulating the response, he shows concern about what Ae-Cha may be feeling.

—SM

5 Listen to How You Speak

Learn to express your feelings calmly and rationally to achieve a more favorable outcome. You don't need to shout and bang your fist on the table when angry (and is this even acceptable or appropriate?) Instead, calmly say something like, 'This makes me feel angry. Let me tell you why'. People will then feel more at ease explaining or attempting to diffuse your anger.

In our experience, a leader who remains consistently calm when expressing disappointment can have a more substantial effect than someone who shouts and rants. Our brains can often feel threatened by things that trigger us resulting in emotional responses. However, when we slow down and remain composed, we capture our listeners' attention. Moreover, this approach also lowers our stress, anxiety, and blood pressure levels.

Your tone and choice of words also make a big difference in how you convey the message. Are you positive? Are you overly positive, which may come across as disingenuous? Are you showing your irritation in a way that is not productive at the moment? Are you clear?

Unless you have very trusting relationships with people who know you well, don't use sarcasm or try to play the devil's advocate. Keep communication clear and direct.

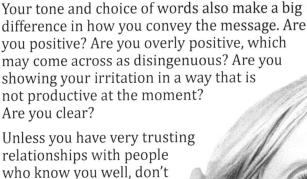

'This above all, to thine own self be true, And it must follow, as the night the day, Thou canst not then be false to any man.'

WILLIAM SHAKESPEARE HAMLET

Think about the behavior you are role modeling. Are you self-motivated? Your behavior could be emulated. Are you focusing on your goals and enjoying what you do? Consider what it is you want to achieve and set yourself some goals. Once you have three or four goals, develop some strategies to help you get there.

6 Set Personal Goals

Connecting your development in emotional intelligence to your goals will be key to your personal growth. In chapter 3, we used a template to encourage you to think about yourself as you start in leadership. Revisit it often and see if your answers change.

Developing goals will help you identify the areas that can enhance your self-awareness and self-management. Take a structured approach in which you set goals for yourself and then devise strategies for achieving these goals by timely executing specific actions.

The strategies provide a more practical understanding of how the goals can be achieved. They are the steps you need to help you reach them. Most technical people are accustomed to developing structured approaches for technical work but only sometimes apply as much structure to their personal development.

When considering the actions that will strengthen the strategy, it is important to ensure they are challenging, distinct, realizable, and appropriate.

Generally, try to develop five or six strategies for each goal.

FROM GEEK TO LEAD
Goal Sheet

MY GOAL

I will learn to manage my anger more effectively.

MY STRATEGY

Understand and become aware of what creates an emotional reaction in me.	Become more aware of how I communicate both verbally and non-verbally.	Realize and accept the feedback is not personal.

MY ACTIONS

Take time to be aware of what types of behavior or comments make me feel angry. (When and by whom I feel triggered.)	If I feel frustrated by a situation or person's behavior, I try to stay calm and not express the negative, not point a finger or blame, but seek to clarify understanding and move to a solution.	Reflect on the outcomes I want from interactions. How I can calm myself by slowing down before I respond.
Think about how I reacted and the outcomes. Also, consider how I feel after an outburst.	Be aware of the tone and volume of my voice.	Raise my awareness of my behavior and reflect. Repeat this at least two or three times a week and review how I changed my thinking.
Write down how I may react differently the next time I feel I am beginning to react.	When I need to express an emotion, do it calmly and establish what I expect, want, or need from the situation.	Be aware of my body language, try to listen, and keep focused.

7 Ask For Help

Becoming more emotionally intelligent means you can boldly ask a more senior experienced leader or mentor to look at your ideas. Together, you can come up with some more practical actions. It will take some time and effort but will ultimately be worthwhile.

Some organizations have performance managers who do not report directly to the leadership team, which can be invaluable. It is a common mistake when taking on a new leadership role to feel that you should know all the answers. It helps to realize that you will make mistakes and not know everything. This is an important self-awareness.

You will make mistakes, but the key is to learn from them. When mistakes happen, think about finding solutions and ways to prevent the problem from recurring instead of blaming yourself or others.

Remember, learning is not enough in itself. It's learning from experience and avoiding repeating the same mistakes that count in the end.

Jot down what you need to know about specific topics and ask others to fill in the gaps. Part of your role as a leader is to mobilize your team to contribute to the knowledge and suggest solutions to the problems—whether technical or not.

By having the team help you with the solutions, not only will you get better answers and increase your own knowledge, but you will also gain their trust and ownership. Many leaders we have worked with have gained great value from working on themselves, increasing their emotional intelligence, and becoming more authentic.

In the next couple of chapters, we look at how you can build on your communication skills and relate to others with an increasing sense of self-awareness.

Leadership is so much more than technical skills.

Relating, connecting and engaging with people is important too.

Be yourself: be authentic.

Develop your self awareness and emotional intelligence.

Your leadership skills will inspire, impact, and influence.

Consistently work on yourself.

Take time to solicit feedback, reflect and learn.

It's who you are as a person, the competencies you develop and your mindset that can support your leadership journey.

THE
ABC
OF
COMM-
UNICATION

Once you
are a leader,
every
conversation
is a
leadership
conversation.

SANDY
MOLLOY

The Power Of Communication

As a leader, you should never underestimate the power of what and how you communicate.

Appropriate communication at all organizational levels can determine the success or failure of leaders or their strategies.

We recently asked several first-time leaders to summarize what they learned from their new role. Expecting to hear various responses, we discovered they all had similar insights.

They responded that their everyday leadership activities, such as success with operations, delivery, delegating, giving feedback, resolving conflicts, and talking to peers and leaders, end users, and the business, all came down to what and how they communicated and how they related to others.

Developing the ability to communicate effectively is one of those critical skills that you need to acquire and continuously build on as a leader.

You will need to relate, adapt, and meet the needs of many different people, as our first-time leaders testified to. *Remember, just be you, but more skilfully.*

This requires refining your communication skills, including your ability to adapt your language, style, and approach in various situations to address different kinds of people. You also need to consider how you are thinking, as your words and actions reflect your mindset.

ABCDEF

THE ABCs OF COMMUNICATION

Many people you will interact with may not be as technically savvy as you or your team. We all have different communication needs and styles. Adapting your communication style and content to their needs is essential to building trust and forming sustainable relationships. Here are the ABCs of Communication, starting with the 3 As.

Know Your
Audience

Get to know the people you communicate with. By understanding your audience better you will be able to plan your communications to get the best results.

Be aware of how others interact, and try to adapt your style so you can communicate in terms of what matters to them. The important consideration is how your message will be received. You will
need to exhibit empathy in some situations, be aware of inclusivity and show people respect to earn their respect.

Keep it
Authentic

When people feel you are being genuine, they will be more inclined to listen to you.

Be honest and direct to achieve better outcomes.

Listen with the intent to understand.

Don't feel you have to use unfamiliar language to appear knowledgeable—be real.

'I do not have the answers, but the answer is in the room.'

OVERHEARD
AT A CIO
CONFERENCE

66

Avoid
Emotional Responses

Avoid people's dramas. Remove yourself from office gossip. Don't be defensive. Refrain from judging or making assumptions. Avoid interrupting, let people speak.

Be aware that casual comments, criticisms, or misplaced jokes are easily misinterpreted.

THE COFFEE THAT SAVED A TEAM

In dealing with increasingly escalating corporate issues, a CIO felt she was drifting away from the team.

She also heard through the grapevine that team members were not feeling appreciated, and the quality of their work was deteriorating.

She realized that her focus on the 'big strategic issues' had isolated her from her team, and she wanted to reconnect with them.

Every week, the CIO set aside an hour and invited a different group of team members to join her for coffee or lunch. She listened to their concerns and talked about work and life in general.

The buzz went around the organization, and the team's productivity increased. Staff started feeling appreciated and their voices heard.

When asked by her colleagues about how she turned the team around, she answered, 'By drinking coffee with them, listening, and being there'.

—YA

COMMUNICATE LIKE A LEADER

Every time you interact with your team, you wear a 'leadership cloak', and your conversations reflect not only yourself but also the management and leadership. It is, therefore, important to be conscious of what you say and how you say it. Here are the Four Bs of Communication.

Be Visible

As a leader, you must ensure that your team members have a strong connection to their work and you as their leader. While you may be tempted to take charge and work on things independently in your first leadership role, it's important to make yourself visible and available to your team.

Taking the time to converse with your team members and getting to know them can be very beneficial.

Being visible is not just something you need to do when you first become a leader, but something you need to maintain throughout your career as a leader.

Be Present

It's also important to be present when you are with people. We have often been told by teams we have coached that some of their leaders multitask while listening to them.

Recently, a team member described how he could see and hear his leader reading and writing emails during a Zoom meeting.

Ronda recently had a promotion to the director of the applications team.

Being a naturally shy person and a novice leader, she worked out of her office trying to manage plans, follow up on deliverables, and get the team motivated.

But she was having a rough time getting the team to respond.

After discussing this with her coach, she tried some activities to get out of her comfort zone.

She made sure that she would pass by team members at the beginning of the day to say good morning and spend a few minutes with team members on her way to and from other meetings.

She also had non-work-related conversations with them.

Slowly, the team response started to change.

They felt acknowledged, which impacted how they perceived her as their leader and not just a manager of tasks.

Their relationship with her had changed.

Ronda was learning that simply acknowledging your team daily with non-work related albeit brief conversations can build rapport. You need to relate, connect, and engage with others.

If it does not come naturally, practice until it becomes a more comfortable habit. —SM

YOU CAN'T CONNECT IF YOU'RE NOT VISIBLE

THE INVISIBLE CLOAK OF LEADERSHIP

The elders of the Northern Kenyan Maasai tribe choose their leaders after observing how they behave daily and in difficult situations over an extended period—sometimes years.

The elders assess how the young warriors live the tribe's values and how they achieve their responsibilities and reach their goals.

The elders highly value the ways in which the young warriors resolve issues and relate to each other.

After the elders meet to decide who will be selected as a leader, they visit the warrior and his family to present the chosen individual with the leadership cloak.

Although a beautifully beaded leather garment, the cloak symbolizes leadership and is only physically worn on special occasions. From that day on, the leader believes that he is wearing the invisible cloak of leadership and that once it has been bestowed upon him, he will always be a leader, and every conversation will be a 'leadership conversation'.

—SM

This raises many questions:

How does this show respect for
the team member?

How does that illustrate
being present?

What message does this
convey to the recipient?

Why have a meeting if you are
not prepared to listen or be
attentive and present?

If the discussion is important, you should be present and actively listening. The brain will focus on whatever you tell it to.

If it is difficult for you to concentrate or have other priorities, postpone the meeting.

But don't forget to reschedule if you postpone. Consistently postponing meetings can make people feel demotivated or undervalued.

Here are some tips to help you be more present:

Be
Generous

Sometimes along with the misconception that you should have all the answers, there is a tendency to believe that you need to be doing most of the talking in conversations with the team.

Beware of the monologue mistake. Yes, you are the leader, and yes, you must make decisions, but spending all of your time with your team listening to your own voice will not help you.

Listen! Give team members and others space to contribute.

Be
Specific

Developing the skill of being specific and succinct in your communication and encouraging your team to do the same will help your interactions to be more productive.

Be specific, crisp, and concise. Get to the point. When you make a statement, think of the 'so what?' What is my thinking in saying this? What outcome do I expect from this conversation?

Being specific and succinct and providing your listener with context can also make listening easier.

Deal with facts, remove emotions from conversations, and avoid going into details. Judging the appropriate level of detail to discuss and with whom is important.

Too much detail can take you off track and cause you to lose track of the 'so what.' It is also important to coach your team to do the same.

'Seek first to understand, then to be understood.'

STEPHEN COVEY

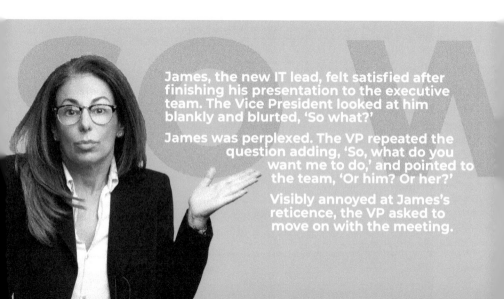

James, the new IT lead, felt satisfied after finishing his presentation to the executive team. The Vice President looked at him blankly and blurted, 'So what?'

James was perplexed. The VP repeated the question adding, 'So, what do you want me to do,' and pointed to the team, 'Or him? Or her?'

Visibly annoyed at James's reticence, the VP asked to move on with the meeting.

So, for example, instead of claiming

> I fight for the rights of my team, and if I see anything that is unfair, I will address it with anyone involved.

Rephrase it so it could be stated as

> I am loyal to my team.

Likewise, instead of saying

> Everything is going wrong; nobody is listening, and the issues are getting out of hand. I am asking people to do things, and they are just not getting done.

Reform it to

> We are off track here. We need to stop now and think about where we are and what to do next.

When you are initially specific and succinct, you can always expand on the details if needed. The listeners can ask you questions, or you can inquire if they want or need more information to help with the discussion.

Start with an economy of words. You can always be generous later.

In the same breath, The VP asked James to leave the room and establish specific action points, expectation, and key takeaways.

James used this learning experience to always ensure his communication is clear, and precisely delineating what needs to be conveyed to the team. And more importantly, what outcomes he expects from his audience.

—SM

WORK ON YOURSELF

Be self-aware and pay attention to how you communicate. Be conscious of what might create a reaction in you or others. As outlined in chapter 4, being aware of how you respond and interact is key. Here are three Cs to get you going.

Communicate

Conscientiously

The fact is that leaders do have to communicate, adapt, and relate to others more visibly and more often, so being prepared for this is an essential part of your role.

If you are a naturally quiet person who finds it difficult to chat with people, participate in small talk (such as social pleasantries unrelated to work), or simply chat spontaneously, engaging with others will require more effort.

However, it is worth it. You will benefit from caring about what other people think, need, or enjoy. People who know you will respect the extra effort you put in, and the more you practice it, the less painful it will become.

Sometimes an individual with introverted preferences, such as processing information internally and thinking things through before talking, may find too much talking unsettling. If this sounds like you, just factor in a time when you can recharge on your own, albeit for a few minutes.

On the other end of the spectrum, you may be outgoing and comfortable talking to anyone, or you may have extrovert preferences, such as feeling comfortable formulating ideas aloud and talking through everything before you process and reflect.

Thinking out loud can often be misconstrued as giving directions, making decisions on the spot, or even appearing indecisive. The team and others might feel an expectation to act on these remarks. They may also feel there is no space for them to contribute, so be aware if you recognize this in yourself and be prepared to shift your thinking about how you engage in interactions.

Consider trying to listen more than you speak and take time to identify the preferences of the people you interact with.

As you work on yourself to become more self-aware, you will also need to be inclusive and accommodate other styles. You are the guide and leader.

OOPS!

I once had to tell one of my team leaders that he was not performing well and that I expected him to improve.

I sat with him for 30 minutes, walking him through all the issues, and I believed I had clearly articulated all my expectations.

After the meeting, a colleague of mine told me that this team leader came out of the meeting with a big smile, telling everyone that he was the best leader I had.

WHAT? It turns out that I used the wrong choice of words.

At the beginning of my meeting with him, I said, 'As one of my top leaders, I expect you to....' And all he heard was, 'As one of my top leaders'.

In retrospect, I should have said, 'As one of my senior leaders, I expect you....'

One word can make a big difference. Choose your words carefully.

—YA

Clarify
and Conquer

Planning how and what you will communicate will improve clarity and the outcomes of your interactions. Additionally, it can help you appear organized and respectful of others' time.

When planning your conversation, ask yourself:

What is the desired outcome?

What do I want to accomplish?

What is the objective of the communication?

One approach is to write down what you want to say before the interaction. Write, rewrite, and then practice your 'talking points'. Make sure your talking points and their order achieve their purpose and tell the story. Writing your talking points down before a meeting can help you clarify your thoughts and allows you to practice your message in a specific and succinct manner.

Be careful, though, not to be so set on your points that you forget to listen!

One important thing, possibly the most important is *'clarity.'*

If you want others to understand the purpose of the interaction, explain it to them and clarify the context.

When we know what to expect, we feel safer. The human brain prefers certainty, and providing context helps people feel more comfortable.

Be clear in your introductions and consider the conclusions. This will help you involve others and clearly understand the next steps to take in terms of action and ownership.

It's Not about You

Don't they say we all have a story in us? If you are telling a story, make sure it is a short story, not a novel, and not always about yourself! We expand on the skill of storytelling later in the book, and you will notice we have also told our own stories to illustrate points and ideas.

Let your listeners develop confidence in you and what you say.

Prepare, Prepare, Prepare

Without this preparation, you may end up rambling —and lose the audience.

You can plan for most interactions. Not the passing in the corridor or chatter with colleagues about the weekend, but key conversations.

Even the most experienced leaders will devote time to plan their conversations carefully. The more you do this, the better you become at identifying the purpose and outcomes required.

Preparing for conversations also lets you consider how you can get the best out of the interaction.

It gives you time to reflect on your knowledge, investigate a new contact, or review any insights you may have had that will help you achieve your desired results. You may not always be able to predict how things will turn out, but you will have a better chance of success with preparation and planning.

WORDS ARE LIKE GODS

'Words are like gods,' said Chief Joseph. He explained what he meant. 'With words, you can create whole new worlds in people's minds. With words, you can make people do anything you want. Use words with care. Craft each thought like a potter, weave each sentence like a weaver, and polish each word like a silversmith.' With that, he fell silent.

This extract was from an interview conducted by Jo Owen in Papua New Guinea as part of his tribal program. Jo has written many leadership books, and we highly recommend you look out for his work. Chief Joseph was knighted by Her Majesty Queen Elizabeth II, for preventing civil war in Papua New Guinea and services to his country. I was also privileged to present with Chief Joseph and spend many delightful hours chatting about leadership. —SM

Capture
the Moment

Taking notes is an excellent skill to develop.

Always keep the notebook with you. If something distracts you, jot it down in your notebook. Clients, team members, or superiors will frequently interrupt you. By keeping a notebook nearby, you can quickly jot down your thoughts, what tasks you need to complete next, and any relevant information that will allow you to pick up where you left off later.

If the timing of the interruption is not appropriate, don't be afraid to ask people to either come back or ask them to be specific and stick to a restricted time. You will find that when people are asked to come back, the issue is often resolved, or they have had time to think more proactively, so it's a good leadership tip.

You will be involved in many conversations during your day, so simply relying on your memory can be difficult. Keeping a notebook allows you to look back at previous meetings and thoughts and pick up where you left off, showing people you were present and listening.

Finally, note that a moment of insight only lasts a fleeting time, and you will be in a busy environment, so writing can reinforce ideas and help shape them.

'If you have an idea, write it down. Until you write it down, you do not have an idea.'

UNKNOWN

HOW GOOD COMMUNICATION SAVED MY CAREER

'I was like a train. I could see what station I was heading for, and all I wanted to do was achieve that goal at any cost. Technical deliverables. My immediate leader was driven in the same way, so my behaviors were not criticized. I did not see any obstacles and got little guidance to change anything. I told myself that I was delivery oriented, and that's what we were there for, to deliver.

'I understood the value of communication, but I was too busy and focused on what I needed to do rather than acknowledge the skills required to be an effective communicator. 'I then got some feedback in a mentoring conversation and got some coaching. At that point, I tried to fix some things about myself. Although I knew that communication, empathy, teamwork, and synergy were key,

and I could talk about their importance, I never practiced those things.

'Slowly I started to fix some poor relationships through honest conversations with my team members, peers, and managers.

'I found that by listening to others and working with them instead of demanding of them, we were achieving results together.

'I also tried to be more transparent and honest and worked hard to understand how others saw things and how to approach others, acknowledging that everyone should be treated with respect.

'Some relationship repairs took just a chat over coffee, while others took more time and harder conversations to rebuild the trust that had been eroded. In becoming more self-aware of some things I had been

blind to, I started to behave differently and consequently got different results.

'I determined to be more proactive and become better at communicating.

'I have stopped labeling myself as delivery oriented and now describe myself as more of a relationship builder. I spend time thinking about how to relate to people and meet their needs. I work on this consciously every day. I see this as an important lesson to learn, and my changes are a personal achievement. I am also getting things delivered!

—SM

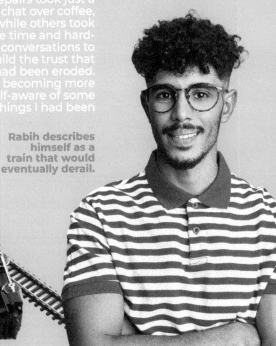

Rabih describes himself as a train that would eventually derail.

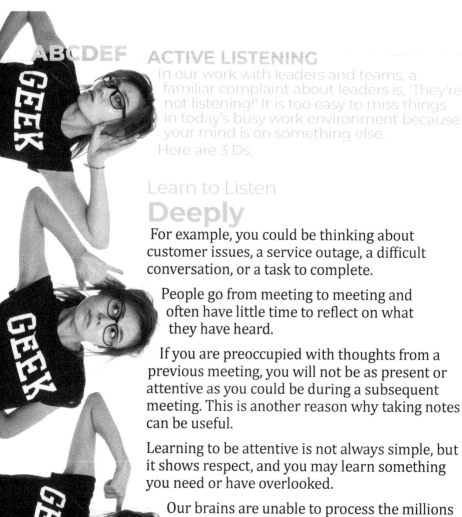

ACTIVE LISTENING

In our work with leaders and teams, a familiar complaint about leaders is, 'They're not listening!' It is too easy to miss things in today's busy work environment because your mind is on something else.
Here are 3 Ds.

Learn to Listen
Deeply

For example, you could be thinking about customer issues, a service outage, a difficult conversation, or a task to complete.

People go from meeting to meeting and often have little time to reflect on what they have heard.

If you are preoccupied with thoughts from a previous meeting, you will not be as present or attentive as you could be during a subsequent meeting. This is another reason why taking notes can be useful.

Learning to be attentive is not always simple, but it shows respect, and you may learn something you need or have overlooked.

Our brains are unable to process the millions of pieces of information they receive every second, so they filter. How we filter can impact what we hear and select to listen to.

Some factors can make it difficult to listen effectively.

Sometimes the way someone speaks can trigger a reaction in us. Their attitude may cause us to mentally disagree without fully understanding their perspective, or we may pick out one of their comments or opinions and start rehearsing our response instead of paying attention to what they're saying. Don't be tempted to build your answers while the other person is talking.

If you tell yourself that listening is difficult or that you find certain people difficult to listen to, your brain will store that as a fact. The subconscious does not distinguish between the truth and a lie, so it's better to make a concerted effort and tell yourself that you will be more attentive and present when listening.

If you listen for problems, you will hear problems. If you are listening with the assumption that you already know the answer, you will stop listening and simply wait for your turn to respond.

This is particularly relevant to technical people who are always looking for a solution. Remember that the brain will deal with what you tell it to focus on.

LISTENING FIXED IT

A new CIO joined an organization at a time when everything was going wrong with IT. The business stakeholders were unhappy, and IT could do nothing right in their eyes. The first thing the new CIO did was to set up regular bi-weekly meetings with each stakeholder to listen to their issues and help address them. During these meetings, the CIO listened intently to the complaints, acknowledged the issues, and let them know when their concerns were legitimate. Although the CIO also supported the team in fixing these concerns, the issues required extensive investment and would take years to resolve. Despite that, after continuing to meet with the stakeholders, the complaints stopped. The stakeholders started trusting the IT team to address the real operational and technical issues because the CIO had been transparent, honest, and listened sincerely.

—YA

Decode

and Decipher

Another key behavior while listening is to focus on what is being said from the 'other person's point of view.' This is empathic.

Put yourself in their shoes to better understand where they are coming from. Listen to understand, not defend your position. Don't forget to give them back their shoes, though!

It becomes more difficult when we listen to similar issues and realize we've heard it all before but must listen as if it's the first time.

Technical people often deal with the same issues repeatedly and may feel they have solved the problem before the person has stopped talking. Try to resist this habit because, for the speaker, it may be their first time facing this issue, and they need to feel that they have your full attention and have been heard.

Listening takes a lot of concentration and energy, especially when we're rushing from meeting to meeting and working with a variety of people, each with their own way of articulating needs, wants, and issues.

But remember, good listening is often used as a measure of how effective a communicator you are. When we genuinely listen to understand what others are saying, it can open up a world of opportunities.

Listening, however, is not always about you having to influence or solve problems (although in the workplace, it is frequently that!). Listen, because it is the right thing to do, to connect and understand another.

Don't
Judge

Focus on what is being said without judgment or assumptions. Read 'The Top Five Essential Listening Tips' on the next pages to help you hone this skill.

'Listen with curiosity. Speak with honesty. Act with integrity. The greatest problem with communication is we don't listen to understand. We listen to reply. When we listen with curiosity, we don't listen with the intent to reply. We listen for what's behind the words.'

Roy T. Bennett

THE TOP FIVE ESSENTIAL
LISTENING

Here are some tips on how to become a better listener:

KEEP EYE CONTACT with the person you are listening to. Even if cultural norms or the speaker's personal discomfort cause them to avoid eye contact, stay focused on them. You don't have to stare, but just relax and focus on the words and how they are expressed.

CLEAR YOUR MIND. Use the clear-the-space technique and be open-minded. Jumping to conclusions or assuming you know where a conversation is headed can lead to misunderstandings or give the impression that you are judging the person rather than actively listening to them.

DON'T INTERRUPT. If you feel the need to, just jot down a note and address it later. Often if you do this and continue listening to the speaker, they will have clarified or covered the point as they continue. Let people finish their train of thought; it helps them to feel listened to.

TIPS

ASK QUESTIONS to clarify and gain more understanding. Some examples might be: 'How did you reach that conclusion?' 'What do you want me to do?' 'How do you want to progress this?' 'So, where do you think we go from here?' The questions will be dependent on the context and situation.

Questions can often help the speaker to clarify things for themselves and sense-check what they have said.

BE AWARE OF YOUR FACIAL EXPRESSIONS and your use of nonverbal cues, such as nodding or making sounds, and think about the words you choose. This can also reflect empathy and acknowledgment of what the speaker is experiencing.

Comments such as 'I can see how that might be confusing for you' or 'I can see you are annoyed by this' shows empathy without judgment.

Start using the checklist provided over the next week. Review three things you have done well—the brain loves numbers—and what you could do differently. Keep practicing.

Repeat. Repeat. Repeat. Listening is not always easy, but it is worthwhile.

Good listening is a habit you can acquire and a key skill valued by others.

LISTENING

TOP 5
- [ ] Keep eye contact.
- [ ] Clear your mind.
- [ ] Do not interrupt.
- [ ] Ask questions.
- [ ] Note facial expressions.

EXTRA CREDIT
- [ ] Stay focused.
- [ ] Filter out distractions.
- [ ] Stay curious.
- [ ] Take and refer to notes.
- [ ] Show empathy.
- [ ] Let go of ego.
- [ ] Capture new learnings.

THE 20 ONE-YEAR LEADER

Michael was a leader with twenty years of experience in various leadership roles.

Early in his career, Michael had attended a series of leadership courses as part of his induction into a global organization.

His mentor was very charismatic but autocratic. This attitude had a powerful impact on what Michael emulated in his first year of leading people.

He carried many attributes from this experience into his future leadership roles.

The only problem was that he became what is called the 20-one-year leader. He tended to repeat what he had absorbed in that first year of induction.

Regardless of the varying expectations and contexts among the people he led, Michael consistently displayed the same behaviors.

Over time, he found it a mystery that he could not get results or motivate his team even though he constantly referred to his first experience as the measure of good leadership.

He had not realized he had stagnated, stopped learning, and simply relived his first year—for the next nineteen years!

He clearly was not self-aware enough to respond to the changing times. He failed to notice his context or read the signs. While he had a charming personality, he gained little respect from his teams over his career. He was immune to understand their pain points and simply failed to respond to any of their genuine concerns.

In basic terms, he was not listening. And neither was he open to receiving feedback, however constructive.

He felt alone, and felt that he was always busy and overworked because he failed to engage the team for support.

Seriously lacking self-awareness, Michael imposed his leadership beliefs onto others, expecting them to conform to his expectations while neglecting to shift his mindset.

Michael, our 20 One-Year leader, missed the opportunity to make great progress in his career. For lack of an empathetic ear and critical self-awareness, Michael had plateaued and thus hampered his growth.

Instead he fell into a permanent state of bewildered stagnation.
—SM

IT'S ONLY WORDS

We have all experienced saying the wrong things or using the wrong words at the wrong moment and have not been pleased with the outcomes! Choosing your words may be easier if you have time to plan things. Keep the 3 Es as a reminder to choose the right words.

sElect
Your Words Wisely

Remember the SPR model: pause, take a breath, think about the outcome you want, be clear, and then respond.

We can often play with words because we do not want to face a contentious situation or are afraid to give offense. But, by being honest and considerate, you can find the right words to express what you need to say clearly.

Your intention should be honorable and transparent. Think about the meaning of the words and how they might be received.

Elucidate
Positively

In his book, *The 7 Habits of Highly Effective People*, Stephen Covey introduces the concept of the proactive individual using proactive, positive language.

'Better to remain silent and be thought a fool than to speak out and remove all doubt.'

ABRAHAM LINCOLN

Reactive language can be emotional, suggest a lack of control, and create a sense of being the victim.

So, remarks such as,

I can't do this.

Nobody is listening.

How am I expected to do this?

There is nothing we can do.

I wasn't given the right information.

and similar sentiments tend to reflect a sense that things are out of the individual's control. It suggests that the user thinks the problem is 'out there', and this type of thinking is a problem.

A leader who uses this type of language will not instill a positive, can-do attitude in their teams, leading to more problems and drama.

Consistently using negative language creates a victim mentality in teams making improvements and feedback more difficult.

Proactive language, on the other hand, involves using more definitive statements, such as,

Let's look at this a different way.

What will it take for us to move this forward?

We will.

OK let's take this step by step.

We can work this through.

and other such words and phrases are more likely to impact the team and increase productivity.

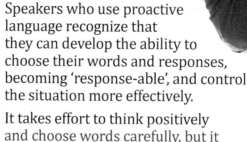

Speakers who use proactive language recognize that they can develop the ability to choose their words and responses, becoming 'response-able', and control the situation more effectively.

It takes effort to think positively and choose words carefully, but it reflects your state of mind.

Here are some tips on how to use proactive, positive language:

Replace *but* with *and* in your conversations. You will notice a difference.

For example, instead of saying

> ❌ The solution seems fine **but** it will take a big team to implement it.

say this

> ✅ The solution seems fine **and** it will take a big team to implement it.

This change allows the words following *and* to build on what has been said rather than sounding like a disagreement, while also allowing the discussion to focus on what needs to be done.

By taking small steps like this every day, you can become more mindful of your words and the impact they may have.

Try nodding, smiling, and using phrases like

> ✅ Absolutely.
> I like that.
> That sounds interesting: Tell me more.

There will be opportunities to slot in phrases like this in your day. As you become more comfortable with this habit, you'll notice more occasions to use uplifting language.

Replace phrases like

> **It was better when...** ✕

with

> It will get easier when... ✓

and replace a statement like

> **Don't do that in the future** ✕

with

> Do make sure next time that you... ✓

When talking about the work environment, use positive words such as ✓

> Engaging.
> Productive.
> Supportive.
> Flexible.
> Generous.
> Collaborative.

When you talk about people, use positive words such as ✓

> Committed.
> Reliable.
> Authentic.
> Transparent.
> Enthusiastic.
> Thoughtful.
> Trustworthy.
> Insightful.
> Supportive.

Listen to your team's language and, if necessary, ask them to rephrase it or bring it up in a one-on-one meeting. This will encourage the team to create a more positive environment.

Every Leader
Is on Stage

You should also be aware that people can misinterpret your nonverbal communication, ie, your body language, which tends to be highly visible. This can impact how they perceive you. Therefore, it's crucial to consistently project positivity and take a proactive approach that reflects your authentic self.

WE FEEL YOUR PAIN

The CEO and several of the team were in an elevator early in the morning.

Someone acknowledged the executive, who grunted an abrupt 'morning' without eye contact or conviction.

As I went into the open plan area, some of the team stopped me to ask if there were any issues with work or problems in the business.

On questioning them, they said the CEO appeared angry and wasn't very friendly.

I popped into his office later and asked him if everything was OK.

I told him about the concerns the people in the elevator had expressed. He grimaced and said, 'Wow, seriously. I get bad headaches and pain in my eyes early in the day because I am being treated for an eye problem. I forgot my eye drops today. Surely, they can't think there's a problem with the business because I don't smile at everyone all the time.'

Staying mindful of these things can help you turn them into habits.

We are not suggesting that you smile all day but that you be aware that your feelings and emotions are visible to others and can impact them.

Similarly, as people become more familiar with your leadership style, they will begin to understand what your body language means and, hopefully, respond accordingly.

We discussed how the staff notices a leader's behavior and how people take their lead from their leaders. We chatted, too, about managing moods and consistency. He noted it!

Later that morning, he walked around the open plan area and chatted with several people smiling and nodding in acknowledgment.

When he felt the positive environment that this created, he started to do this more often.

—SM

RUNNING MEETINGS

When you prepare for meetings, ensure you are not running all of them like a status meeting, as these can switch people off once they have presented their own area. Ask yourself, 'How do I want the participants to feel during and after the meeting?' Help people to be clear about what their contributions might be and what is expected of them.

Forge
the Agenda

Be clear about the objective. If someone else is leading the meeting without an agenda or context, ask them, 'What are we wanting to achieve in this meeting?' Ensure your meetings have agendas and that you have considered the messages and outcomes you want.

If you do hold status meetings, ensure that you only discuss the top three issues or priorities and that, if input from others is required to advance your plans, you leave some 'white space' on the agenda to discuss unrelated but still useful topics.

Follow
the Agenda

Everyone's time is precious. Be aware of the time allotted. Place key topics or issues at the start of the conversation and be aware of the clock. We run out of time for many reasons, but sometimes important communications can be missed. We've heard people leave meetings complaining about wasted time or people who dominate discussions

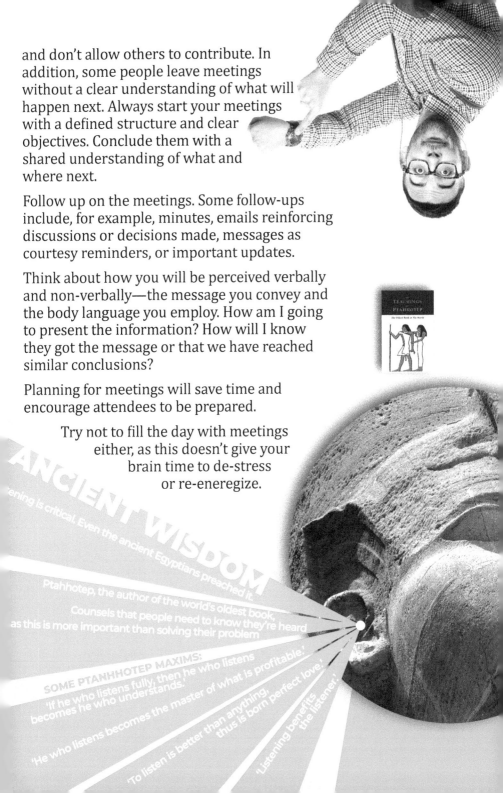

and don't allow others to contribute. In addition, some people leave meetings without a clear understanding of what will happen next. Always start your meetings with a defined structure and clear objectives. Conclude them with a shared understanding of what and where next.

Follow up on the meetings. Some follow-ups include, for example, minutes, emails reinforcing discussions or decisions made, messages as courtesy reminders, or important updates.

Think about how you will be perceived verbally and non-verbally—the message you convey and the body language you employ. How am I going to present the information? How will I know they got the message or that we have reached similar conclusions?

Planning for meetings will save time and encourage attendees to be prepared.

Try not to fill the day with meetings either, as this doesn't give your brain time to de-stress or re-eneregize.

ANCIENT WISDOM

...ening is critical. Even the ancient Egyptians preached it.

Ptahhotep, the author of the world's oldest book,

Counsels that people need to know they're heard as this is more important than solving their problem

SOME PTANHHOTEP MAXIMS:

"If he who listens fully, then he who listens becomes he who understands."

"He who listens becomes the master of what is profitable."

"To listen is better than anything, thus is born perfect love."

"Listening benefits the listener."

Focus

Focus, Focus

Telling yourself to stop thinking about anything other than the situation at hand sends a signal to your brain. Keep repeating 'Clear the space' to yourself in your head or aloud.

You may not have much time between meetings, but it only takes a few seconds to tell your brain to focus. Clearing the space is a simple but effective message to say to yourself. Be in the moment!

You can also suggest this during team meetings so everyone is prepared to listen.

If someone has something urgent or troubling to say, which prevents them from being present, let them say it, and you can decide whether to take it up or leave it.

Making sure you and others are present and have cleared their minds will save time and help you focus.

What's Next

Take the time to improve yourself and your communication skills; they are important lifelong skills.

In the next chapter, we will look at how being aware of how others communicate and how you self-regulate/manage your communications will create opportunities for more effective interactions.

So, now that we've spent some time looking at how you can become more self-aware and fine-tune your communication, let's look at how you can relate and communicate with others.

Leadership is all about communication. It is a critical skill for leaders.

Get to know your team.

Be visible, be present and be receptive.

Listen, really listen.

Plan what you want to communicate in your interactions and provide clarity.

Increase self-awareness of how you communicate most effectively.

Be authentic and project a positive proactive attitude.

Remember every conversation you have as a leader is a leadership conversation.

KEY
IDEAS
CHAPTER
5

INTERACTING WITH OTHERS

Up to a point you welcome being interrupted because it is only by interacting with others that you get anything done.

KEN ROBINSON

Developing Positive Interactions

In the digital world today, we are seeing many changes in the workplace. Remote and hybrid working, the sharing of roles, reduced working hours, the abundance of emails, zoom calls, online team meetings, a variety of social media, and new generations of employees with different expectations, are becoming the norm. The ability to communicate and interact with others has become an even more critical leadership competency.

IT leaders are often called on to step in and resolve issues with end users and stakeholders not related to technical issues, but because of the way the team members have communicated with them.

Because your teams will be made up of people who prefer different communication styles, you must encourage them to build on their strengths while respecting and working on their differences with others.

As a leader, it is vital that you develop positive interactions and relationships. We are not being idealistic and suggest that everyone can relate well to everyone else, but you should make every effort to engage in positive interactions, as often as you can, across the organization. Hopefully this is something you will have learned and practiced long before you took on the role of leader. Remember to be real too. Be authentic.

'Perpetual optimism is a force multiplier— the ripple effect of a leader's enthusiasm and optimism is awesome. So is the impact of cynics and pessimism. Leaders who whine and blame engender those same behaviors among their colleagues.'

GENERAL
COLIN
POWELL

Build Respectful Relationships

In the 1994 film *Forrest Gump*, a film primarily about respect and tolerance, the main character Forrest famously says, 'Life is like a box of chocolates. You never know what you're gonna get.' The workplace is similar, with different personal aspirations, personalities, genders, cultural backgrounds, values, and expectations of the employees.

It is key, that as a leader, you build trusting and mutually respectful relationships: with team members, acting as a role model, with peers, with whom you will need to build collaborative relationships, and with your business clients, end users, and many others.

Building positive relationships is a key component of creating your organization's culture. Good interactions will enhance your well-being and that of those around you. It will also reflect how others perceive you, your teams, and IT as a willing and trusted business partner. Some interactions will be more important than others and have more impact on the business or people. There will be key relationships.

However, you can also keep a positive outlook on all your communications, even if some are only brief or transactional.

It takes time to build relationships, to connect, relate to and engage with others, but once you have connected, give it time. It's a skill you need to foster from the start of your working life. Some people, however, might find it easier to relate to others. It's almost a gift for some, while for others, it is less comfortable and may take more effort and courage. Working at it will be worthwhile.

Once you have connected with others, take the initiative, and follow up. It is important for you to reach out to different people and develop relationships with skillful interactions.

Seek Out Opportunities to Connect

Seek out opportunities to connect with people you need to influence or serve. Sharing information and knowledge, both in your team and in the business community, can help people feel more connected with each other and result in more satisfying working relationships.

With increased remote working, it is also important that you take the initiative to communicate with your remote workers. You can decide on which media to use, depending on the context of the interaction, but try to find out how people are feeling and keep them informed of what is going on in the office.

We recently spoke to a new leader who decided to switch around

video and audio meetings to encourage the team to listen and interact differently with different approaches. He also encouraged a rotation of the chair and development of the agenda to encourage participation and variety.

When you're implementing a hybrid work setup where people work from home and in the office, you will have some participants joining meetings remotely. In such situations, it's easy for remote participants to feel left out as the people in the room chat with each other, leaving only one or two people greeting the online attendees. It is more inclusive to get everyone in the room to acknowledge the people calling in and make them feel welcomed into that environment. Some remote workers are missing the daily small talk interactions.

'I fear the day technology will surpass our human interaction. The world will have a generation of idiots.'

ALBERT EINSTEIN

Relating well to others in the workplace, your team, and the business can be rewarding. If you're passionate about what you do and what and how you deliver, then developing trusting and sustainable relationships can boost motivation and productivity. You don't want to force a level of intimacy, but there are a few things you can do and be aware of that will help you to relate better to others.

Small Talk Is a Big Deal

In the last chapter, we read about a new leader, Ronda, who preferred to work in her office on task management instead of being present and visible to her team. This was partly because Ronda was shy, and felt uncomfortable with the social pleasantries, preferring to get on to the task at hand. The problem with this is that some people value these everyday interactions as a way of building relationships with others.

Although some people are task-oriented and prefer to jump right in, it's generally better to be personable upfront and use this approach as a default until you learn what the person is comfortable with. However, be socially aware as this can vary with the culture of different countries.

'If you want to change the way people respond to you, change the way you respond to people.'

TIMOTHY LEARY

THE BRAZILIAN CLIENT • AND SOCIAL PLEASANTRIES •

The IT department in the UK had been working on a large project to be delivered to a Brazilian client. The IT team had been developing positive relationships with their counterparts in Brazil.

The head of the business unit went to meet the client. He had prepared his input for the meetings and had an agenda for their first meeting.

The following day the sales consultant got a call from the Brazilian client saying how unhappy he was with the leader's approach to the work. He felt the relationship was impaired and was unhappy.

It took the salesman some time to recover the conversation, and they agreed that another team member, who had been on calls with this client, would be the single point of contact for the technical areas.

So, what went wrong? Apparently, when the senior leader arrived, the client wanted to go for a meal, chat about his family and his town and have some social interactions. The leader was uncomfortable and kept trying to put this agenda forward and talk about work. The client thought this was rude. He had made time available later that afternoon and the next morning to go through the delivery and testing schedules. This was a social interaction to develop a mutually respectful relationship.

You must be socially aware — and, in this case, culturally sensitive—and read the circumstances you find yourself in.

—SM

Different Strokes for Different Folks

You won't need to study psychology to recognize that people communicate differently. You will encounter a wide range of styles in the workplace and in your leadership interactions. If you develop social awareness (as well as developing your self-awareness) it can help you gain a better understanding of how people are feeling and how you might communicate more confidently and clearly with them.

Learn as much as you can about yourself, the people you lead, and those you will be interacting with.

Working with Differences

Your team members will have a variety of communication styles. You may work with quiet team members who prefer to work through their ideas by reflecting on them. They may wait to gather as much required information as possible before contributing.

Some of these individuals may be shy and uncomfortable with drawing attention to themselves.

How will you draw them out?

Then, there are those people who prefer to communicate by talking to help them think through things. They can be expressive and vocal and openly discuss issues and ideas.

'Our worst fault, is our preoccupation with the faults of others.'

KAHLIL GIBRAN

DIFFERENCES WORKING WITH

DRAWING OUT THE
QUIET
TEAM MEMBERS

Don't focus on their silence in public. You can ask for their contributions. However, it would be helpful to inform them of the meeting's agenda or expectations ahead of time. Keep in mind that noisy meetings can overwhelm the quieter members of the team. Don't feel uneasy about moments of silence or pauses as they gather their thoughts.

Don't judge this style of communication. It is important that you don't encourage the more outgoing people to push the quieter ones into 'speaking up'. This just makes them feel more awkward.

Give them time. The quiet person often needs time to process their thoughts.

After they have processed and gathered the energy to speak, **don't dismiss their contribution** too quickly. Doing so will impair their engagement.

If it's possible, **give the quiet people space** and even a work environment that allows them to recharge.

Others may simply be shy and enjoy being with people but don't feel like speaking out. But they are in the moment too. However, **don't assume their silence is consent.** It might be easier to gain their commitment in a one-to-one interaction.

It may benefit their development by **encouraging them to leave their comfort zone** but **be careful not to create anxiety** in your quieter team members.

DEALING WITH THE MORE
OUTSPOKEN
TEAM MEMBERS

Trust that they act in the team's best interests by sharing their ideas and thoughts.

Don't be judgmental. Acknowledge their contribution but firmly bring their involvement to an end to **allow others to participate.**

Some people think out loud. To reduce this verbal brainstorming, structure your conversations, **keep them focused** by answering specific questions, and deal with facts, not opinions.

Encourage the enthusiasm and energy of your team, but also **encourage them to be specific and succinct** without making them feel as if their input is being devalued. It's good to have a mix of styles and personalities in your teams.

There are differences between loud and opinionated speakers and extroverts who love discussing ideas and sharing their thoughts. Extroverts love interactions, meetings, and exchanging stories with others. **Don't shut them down** but encourage them to be socially aware of the differences in how others react and how to adapt.

If you **encourage them to develop their emotional intelligence,** they can respond positively by sharing their stage.

A leadership consultant was engaged in a project and tasked with working with another consultant for a key client.

Within minutes of the meeting, she realized that they approached things differently.

She was extremely outgoing, sharing ideas, some of which came to mind as she spoke.

He was noticeably quiet and did not express emotion, but then he produced a very structured document.

While she had assumed (without checking!) that this was an informal meet-up, he behaved as if it was a formal meeting.

She knew then that they would find working together tough unless they addressed how they approached things.

Fortunately, operating in the same field of expertise gave them the opportunity to raise these differences at the end of the meeting.

Working differently from the style that you are used to takes time and energy.

They agreed to accommodate one another by identifying the strengths of their respective styles.

He agreed to listen more attentively to her bouncing around ideas, and she agreed to try to structure things in a way that he could respond to.

They worked hard at this process and, after some time, very much enjoyed working together—much to the amusement of their colleagues, who could see how vastly different they were.

—SM

OPPOSITES ATTRACT

Others may simply enjoy their own voice and opinions, believing that everything they contribute is valuable.

How can you ensure they allow others to contribute without feeling devalued themselves?

You will also work with people who clarify their thoughts by writing things down and prefer structured communications. Others, on the other hand, may need to be encouraged to put their ideas into writing.

It can often be difficult to persuade a busy technical person to write things down, but doing so can help avoid redundant work and increase shared knowledge.

How can you encourage them to document?

As a leader, you can support your team members in developing their strengths while also working on areas where they may be less confident. This is helpful in their personal growth as well as the growth of the team and the business.

ENCOURAGING TECHNICAL PEOPLE TO DOCUMENT

TECHNICAL PEOPLE ARE NOT ALWAYS KEEN TO SIT DOWN AND DOCUMENT. THEY WOULD RATHER BE OUT THERE DOING AND FIXING AND FINDING SOLUTIONS. BE AWARE OF THE LANGUAGE YOU USE TO ENCOURAGE THEM TO DOCUMENT.

Rather than,

'This has to be done, where is it?' ✕

Use positive reinforcement, for example, ✓

'We need to share your knowledge and give you credit for it.'

'The team needs your support.'

'The business is going to appreciate this, and it will make our lives easier.'

If the task seems daunting, break it down into smaller activities. It may feel like a chore, but not all tasks are equally satisfying. Help the team members plan priorities for this activity. Make it part of their performance goals.

Documentation is not a byproduct of IT. It can reduce calls for technical support. The end user may not always be interested in reading a document. Still, collaborative documentation development can be invaluable for capturing knowledge and obtaining advice from subject matter experts. There may also be opportunities to delegate a portion of the development of a document.

There is a myriad of documents in IT, systems administration, product requirements, source code, and maintenance guides, to name a few. But encouraging your technical teams to document will save time and reduce waste resources. It greatly benefits operations and the business as a whole.

Let's have a look at a common workplace communication issue we have all encountered.

We All Make Assumptions

Most of us have been guilty of making assumptions or jumping to conclusions too readily, often resulting in confused communications or crossed wires. Businesses are busy places, we may think we've heard things repeatedly, or we get fatigued or frustrated, or we think we know what the other person will say or deduce.

A useful tool we have often used when talking to leaders and their teams is called The Ladder of Inference. It's a model developed by Chris Argyris, a co-founder of the field of Organizational Development, and later featured in Peter Senge's, *The Fifth Discipline Fieldbook.*

This model illustrates how simple it is to make assumptions and draw conclusions from them, influencing our choice of action. The ladder depicts the unconscious thinking process we all go through, from what we believe to be facts to making decisions and acting.

Problems arise when we bypass certain steps in the process due to our beliefs or past experiences. We jump up the ladder. This can lead us to selectively choose some data and ignore others. We then make inferences and draw conclusions based on assumptions shaped by our past experiences.

Truth is Relative

Often our ability to achieve the desired results is eroded by the feeling that those beliefs are the truth. This truth is obvious to us and, therefore, should be obvious to others. We perceive that our beliefs are based on real data and that the data

'It ain't what you know that gets you into trouble. It's what you know for sure, that just ain't so.'

MARK TWAIN

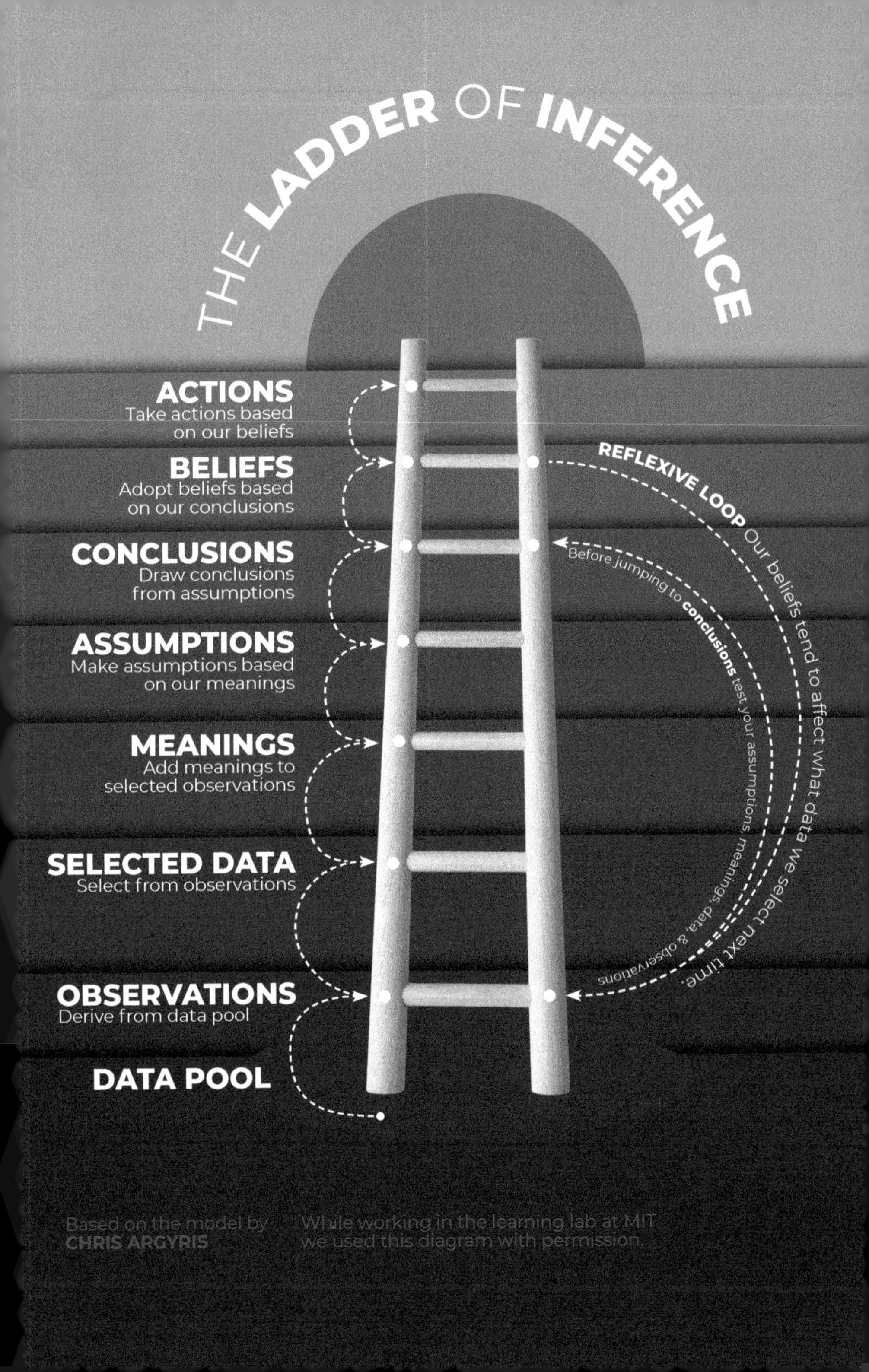

THE LADDER OF INFERENCE

ACTIONS
Take actions based
on our beliefs

BELIEFS
Adopt beliefs based
on our conclusions

CONCLUSIONS
Draw conclusions
from assumptions

ASSUMPTIONS
Make assumptions based
on our meanings

MEANINGS
Add meanings to
selected observations

SELECTED DATA
Select from observations

OBSERVATIONS
Derive from data pool

DATA POOL

REFLEXIVE LOOP Our beliefs tend to affect what data we select next time.

Before jumping to **conclusions** test your assumptions, meanings, data, & observations

Based on the model by
CHRIS ARGYRIS

While working in the learning lab at MIT
we used this diagram with permission.

we select is real. We assert something to be true and factual, only to find out later that we did not have the whole story, that we misinterpreted some information, that we were biased, or that we were simply not listening carefully.

However, we can become more aware of our thinking and reasoning if we consider how we reached those conclusions. We can reflect. We can ask ourselves questions.

Once we've raised that self-awareness, we can make that apparent to others. We can explain our thinking and how we reached a particular conclusion, and we can inquire about the reasoning and thought processes of others to better understand what they are trying to communicate.

This process will help us have more productive conversations. It will save time and avoid misunderstandings. You may have to admit you were wrong.

CLIMBING
THE
LADDER OF
INFERENCE
IN **REAL LIFE**

A training consultant was facilitating a workshop with a team having issues with how they were relating to each other. The meeting started at 9 am.

<OBSERVATIONS>
Philip came in 30 minutes late. He plumped down and made a fair amount of noise as he settled into the room. <SELECTED DATA>
Karen, the team leader, was annoyed that Philip was so late. She felt that Philip was rude to arrive late and interrupt

Slow Down the Process

When you are interacting with others, slow down the process, listen without jumping to conclusions, and test your own and others' assumptions.

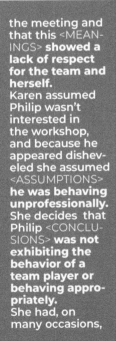

the meeting and that this <MEANINGS> **showed a lack of respect for the team and herself.** Karen assumed Philip wasn't interested in the workshop, and because he appeared disheveled she assumed <ASSUMPTIONS> **he was behaving unprofessionally.** She decides that Philip <CONCLUSIONS> **was not exhibiting the behavior of a team player or behaving appropriately.** She had, on many occasions,

explained to the team how she felt about punctuality <BELIEFS> **stressing that not being on time was disrespectful to her and others on the team.** She felt that Philip should receive feedback that would send a message to the rest of the team. She stopped the meeting and <ACTIONS> **told Philip she was not impressed with his behavior** or his attitude, coming into the meeting so late and disrupting it.

Other team members were uncomfortable. Philip exploded.

He assumed she knew there had been an issue with the client's payroll system the night before for payments due the morning of this meeting. He and two engineers were fixing the problem most of the night, finishing the fix at 4:30 am. He had then gone home to sleep a little and woke up late. He rushed back into the office to attend the session.

For the facilitator, it was magic. There in the room was the ladder in practice in real-time. Both parties here went straight up the ladder. If they had paused to explain or question one another, this awkward interaction could have been much more productive much sooner.

Going up the ladder can happen quickly, and being at the top of it without checking the data and assumptions can be costly in terms of time, productivity, and relationships. —SM

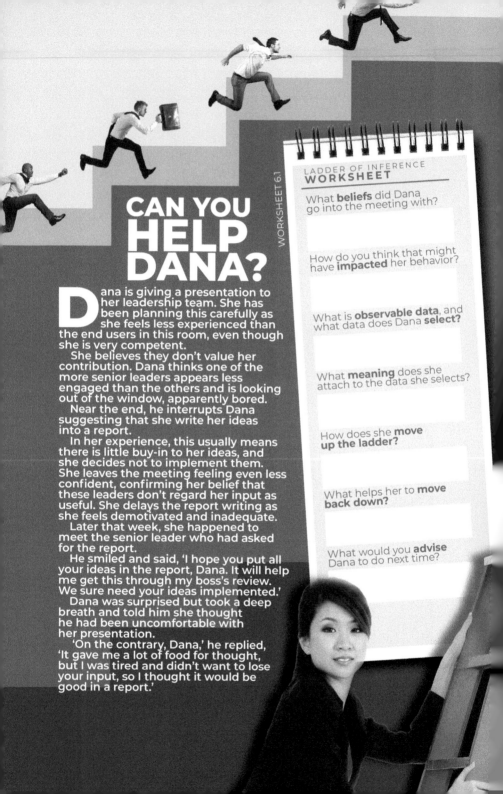

CAN YOU HELP DANA?

Dana is giving a presentation to her leadership team. She has been planning this carefully as she feels less experienced than the end users in this room, even though she is very competent.

She believes they don't value her contribution. Dana thinks one of the more senior leaders appears less engaged than the others and is looking out of the window, apparently bored.

Near the end, he interrupts Dana suggesting that she write her ideas into a report.

In her experience, this usually means there is little buy-in to her ideas, and she decides not to implement them. She leaves the meeting feeling even less confident, confirming her belief that these leaders don't regard her input as useful. She delays the report writing as she feels demotivated and inadequate.

Later that week, she happened to meet the senior leader who had asked for the report.

He smiled and said, 'I hope you put all your ideas in the report, Dana. It will help me get this through my boss's review. We sure need your ideas implemented.'

Dana was surprised but took a deep breath and told him she thought he had been uncomfortable with her presentation.

'On the contrary, Dana,' he replied, 'It gave me a lot of food for thought, but I was tired and didn't want to lose your input, so I thought it would be good in a report.'

LADDER OF INFERENCE
WORKSHEET

What **beliefs** did Dana go into the meeting with?

How do you think that might have **impacted** her behavior?

What is **observable data**, and what data does Dana **select?**

What **meaning** does she attach to the data she selects?

How does she **move up the ladder?**

What helps her to **move back down?**

What would you **advise** Dana to do next time?

BE
SELF-
AWARE
WHEN YOU'RE CLIMBING
THE LADDER OF INFERENCE.

LADDER OF INFERENCE
TOOLKIT

Ask yourself and then ask other people these questions:

How did I/you/we reach that conclusion?

Is it based on facts?

How am I/are you/we interpreting those facts?

What are we basing that conclusion on specifically?

What evidence am I/are you/we focused on?

What made me/you/us choose this course of action?

Have I/you/we excluded other options?

Have I/you/we made any assumptions here?

Are they based on beliefs? Past experiences?

Have I/you/we verified them?

You do not need to mention the ladder, which would turn people off and seem unnatural. Still, by using inquiry and advocating your reasoning (where appropriate), you can outline your thinking and any thinking errors leading you and others to interpret or misinterpret information.

THIS TOOL CAN BE INVALUABLE WHEN BECOMING AWARE OF HOW OTHERS COMMUNICATE.

We all make assumptions, and when we make them, we can reach conclusions in a second. Some of these assumptions are harmless, but others can lead to misinterpretations and mistakes and cost us time and relationships. Going up that ladder can happen without us being aware, so how can we change this behavior?

—SM

Keeping the ladder in mind when interacting with others is also useful in creating shared understanding. It also helps to take the emotion out of many conversations.

The more you do this, the more people will expect you to behave in this way, and the better prepared they will be to answer and ask questions about their thinking and reasoning. Asking questions to gain a better understanding will help you identify any gaps between your thinking and the thinking of others.

You will face difficult conversations in your workplace, but if you can think about the Ladder in your discussions, it can become an extremely healthy tool.

Communicate Proactively and Positively

In the last chapter, we talked about using positive language. Now, let's consider being proactive and its relation to being positive.

You may work with people preoccupied with all the problems around them, even if they cannot solve them. Operating in this area is referred to as the Circle of Concern.

Sometimes the problems people are worried about are beyond their ability to resolve, and worrying about these matters does not help them move forward.

SENDING MESSAGES SIMPLY

Mark is a new leader who recently told us that he had just met with all his team for the first time.

Others had told him that a particular individual was not a team player and not engaged as much in the team. He met this person and found him very excited about technology.

Mark felt that there was potential in him that was being missed. Mark's own leader also dismissed this team member in a meeting.

Mark smiled and, without defending him or disagreeing, chose instead to say, "He reminds me of an excited puppy who just needs some guidance and training. In fact, I recommend that he attend this training sooner rather than later, and then he can engage the team in what he has learned. Puppies calm down with good training and clear direction, and I am happy to work with him."

He didn't need to say anything else, and his leader accepted his analogy. —SM

COMMUNICATIONS CHECKLIST

Here is a checklist to help you reflect on and plan your communications.

- [ ] Listen more, speak less.
- [ ] Be specific and succinct. Generosity of detail and information can follow when appropriate.
- [ ] Plan and prepare.
- [ ] Listen to understand first.
- [ ] Choose words carefully to create shared understanding.
- [ ] Be aware of your and others' assumptions.
- [ ] Balance inquiry (asking the questions) and advocacy (explaining your thinking and reasoning) to reach better outcomes.
- [ ] Keep a positive outlook by using positive language.
- [ ] Consider how and whom you can influence, and if not you, who?
- [ ] Be an example, a role model.
- [ ] Acknowledge and work with other people's styles and strengths.
- [ ] Add storytelling to your tool kit.
- [ ] Refer to the checklist regularly to see what progress you are making, what you are learning, and what you are doing well.
- [ ] Ask trusted peers or colleagues to give you feedback.
- [ ] If you keep a notebook, you can record your findings too.

Focus on Your Influence

If we get into the habit of focusing on things that we cannot control, we lose our power to act or make changes and become less effective.

PROACTIVE
FOCUS

POSITIVE ENERGY
ENLARGES
CIRCLE OF INFLUENCE

REACTIVE
FOCUS

NEGATIVE ENERGY
SHRINKS
CIRCLE OF INFLUENCE

Reactive people focus on things that are in their **Circle of Concern** but not in their **Circle of Influence.** This can lead to blaming external factors, creating negative energy, and causing their Circle of Influence to shrink.

We may not eliminate concern, but we can limit its impact on us and others by shifting our thinking. The better place to operate is within the Circle of Influence.

When we focus on the Circle of Influence, we become proactive, taking the initiative—in other words, we look at and work on the things we can do something about.

The IT department will be expected to find solutions to and ways around problems. However, if you sit with your clients in their Circle of Concern, it will exacerbate the problems and create more intense reactions. Repeating the same issues feels like you are going around in circles! We look at ways you might avoid this in the last chapter.

If your energy goes into things you cannot change, your Circle of Influence will shrink. Not only will you drain your energy, but other people may also start to see you as unnecessarily negative and critical.

Activate Your Circle of Influence

Ensuring you operate in your Circle of Influence will enable you to help others operate in your space. The key is to focus your energy on those things that you can influence, allowing you to make effective changes.

The positive energy we exert will cause our Circle of Influence to expand. This is a proactive mindset. Proactive, positive people constantly increase their Circle of Influence.

We mentioned earlier the need for non-technical leaders to find people who know the technical answers. Asking domain experts and others helps them to increase their Circle of Influence. It is advantageous for technical leaders to work on this as well and remember that the team can have a greater influence than an individual. This demonstrates why networking is such an important skill. When you form partnerships and alliances, you may not have direct influence, but you may know people who do, which increases your impact.

Extending your Circle of Influence is an important aspect of personal effectiveness.

Apply Transactional Analysis
Another useful concept to be aware of when interacting with others is a theory developed by Dr Eric Berne. Originally used for a psychology study, Transactional Analysis (TA) has been adapted for training in business management.

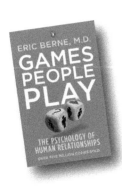

It is, at its heart, a complex topic, but we can simplify it so that it can be added to your leadership tool kit. It is a highly effective method of promoting personal growth and change, helping you to raise self-awareness about how you interact with others.

Berne states that we all operate in one or the other of **three ego states.** An ego state is a way we experience the world and how we relate to others. At times, we can operate in all three ego states. However, by becoming aware of how we think, conduct exchanges with people, and our life experiences, we can learn to adjust our ego state to operate from the most productive one during a particular interaction.

Three Ego States

The ego states are:

PARENT ADULT CHILD

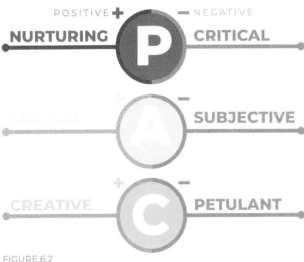

POSITIVE **+** — NEGATIVE

NURTURING — **P** — **CRITICAL**

— **A** — **SUBJECTIVE**

CREATIVE — **C** — **PETULANT**

FIGURE 6.2
THREE EGO STATES
FROM ERIC BERNE

The **Parent** ego state is divided into a nurturing parent and a critical parent. In the Parent ego state, we think, feel, and behave as our real parents or carers did when we were children.

The Adult ego state, which Berne suggests is a psychologically healthier place to operate from, is based on the here and now, the current reality, and it tends to be logical and objective.

The Child ego state plays back our feelings and thoughts as children. A child can be rebellious or petulant or adaptive (hoping to please) and both Parent and Child states tend to be based on the past. People sulking or over reacting are framing their behavior with a child ego state.

Amos [**A**] is having an exchange with Bruce [**B**], his team leader. Bruce had just polished up a proposal before Amos is able to deliver it to a major client. The stakes are high.

A: 'Just so you know, Bruce, I've had to make several corrections as I found typos. I couldn't have sent it out that way.' Amos expresses a **critical parent** tone.

B: 'Well, you've also handed me work that needed a lot of reworking!' Bruce is defensive and sounds like a **petulant child.**

Clearly, this unconstructive pattern is inevitably going to escalate into an ineffective interaction.

Let's replay it.

A: 'I've gone over this document, Bruce. I just changed a couple of spellings, and we're ready to go.' Amos uses an **Adult, non-critical** tone, simply stated with care.

B: 'Thanks, Amos, I'll be more careful next time.' Bruce is communicating in an **Adult** tone which helps them move forward positively.

—SM

Surviving a Critical 'Parent'

We both worked with a leader who consistently acted as a Critical Parent. He used to raise his voice and have exchanges like,

'I'm not at all happy with the work done on this project so far. It's not good enough, and I won't accept it. Who owns this? Why was this done like this?'

Does this remind you of being told off by a parent? A critical parent? Some of the team members began operating in an adaptive child ego state and staying quiet (to survive the onslaught and appear to please the parent), while others became like rebellious children blaming everyone else.

We once heard people leaving one such meeting, saying they had no intention of doing what was asked or demanded of them, and the team slowly became dysfunctional. Information was withheld for fear of the consequences and the team started to fracture.

By operating in a critical parent ego state, the leader was not listening, not asking questions, and constantly making assumptions. He was neither getting the best out of his people nor operating in an adult-to-adult manner.

Surviving a Nurturing 'Parent'

We don't need critical or nurturing parents in the workplace. The second part of the Parent ego state is the Nurturing Parent ego state, and it manifests itself through behavior that is geared toward smoothing things over at all costs and ensuring people are feeling good and things are fair. A person operating in this ego state wants to help and please people. All of this is reasonable in and of itself, but it's also often said that you cannot please all the people all the time. If you say yes to everything you may not be able to deliver, and avoiding conflict or disagreements by acquiescing will create more problems down the line.

The Adult state is the most preferable state to operate in, and using clear, skillful communication, without emotional outbursts, can make exchanges more effective. The Adult will not blame or be critical of others, will look at issues proactively, and will try to find win-win solutions.

Antique bowl repaired with gold to fill the cracks, using Kintsugi, the ancient Japanese restoration technique that celebrates the beauty of imperfections.

FROM BROKEN CERAMICS TO FIXED RELATIONSHIPS

A team workshop facilitator was working with a leadership team, and it became obvious that two of the leaders had issues with each other. They were saying things to her such as,

'I can't work with this person after how she has behaved,'

'I don't think I can trust this guy ever again.'

Rather than deal with this directly, the facilitator decided to tell the whole team in a meeting about the Japanese art of ceramic bowl repair called **Kintsugi.** It is the ancient art of repairing cracked bowls with gold. It is based on the philosophy that nothing is ever broken beyond repair. Gold creates a new beauty that is quite different from before. She then related this to relationships in the team, pointing out that using reactive or emotional language can create barriers to resolving conflicts and come across as definitive or rigid. One of the leaders was struck by the concept of kintsugi and suggested to their colleagues that they look for better ways of working together. A few days later, the two leaders discussed their aspirations for the future and how they could alter their working relationship and communication. —SM

Telling Stories

When Steve Jobs worked at Pixar in 1994, he famously said, 'The most powerful person in the world is the storyteller. The storyteller sets the vision, values, and agenda of an entire generation to come.' Jobs learned this after making some spectacular mistakes early on in his career, but he chose to use the power of the story to inspire so many to go forward.

Steve Jobs
1955 2011

Storytelling is a useful leadership tool. We're not saying you will become another Steve Jobs (or you may one day!) but using a story can keep conversations positive and be part of your ability to influence a situation or other people.

In telling a story, you can engage your audience differently from the norm because you are not telling them what to do. Rather, you allow them to make comparisons, relate what you say to their situation, and come to their own conclusions and insights.

Using metaphors and giving examples in your stories of similar scenarios can often leave the listener thinking differently as they appreciate your point.

A Story about Complainers

Here is an example of how telling a story helped to engage a team in making a change in their behavior. This team had been treated quite poorly in the past, with leaders coming and going. They were left uninformed and lacked clarity about their roles in the team. They were criticized by their end users and spent an excessive amount of time complaining about their situation. They were stuck in a Circle of Concern.

They then got a new leader, and he restructured the team, creating different leadership lines with clear goals and accountabilities. However, the complaining continued. It seems it had become a habit, a part of the team culture.

WE SHALL NOT COMPLAIN

We were working with an IT team known for their negativity.

At the start of one of the days we were working together, we gave each of the attendees a badge to wear that said, "We will not complain."

There was so much laughter and friendly joking about certain people needing several badges, and the team suggested that offenders pay a fine and buy the coffee.

People could hear each other's comments and tones, echoing critical parent and child ego states, because they were becoming self-aware.

This enabled open discussions, and some real changes started to evolve.

Complaining had permeated the culture of the IT organization, and this was another step forward in creating a more positive and productive environment.
—SM

COMPLAINING IN KENYA

On our trips to Kenya, we knew from experience that things would get tough. There was little fresh water, and what there was had to be used for cooking and chai (tea), not for hair washing or showers.

We went there to build schools and water tanks, and we needed to start work early to have more time when the temperature was lower. It got extremely hot as the day progressed, and we worked until the sun went down. Work was physically demanding, and we slept on hard, dry ground tents in the camp. We shared the space with many insects too!

Complaining would have benefited no one. In any way!

So, we agreed with the teams we took out to Kenya that "we would not complain," and they signed their names on a piece of paper.

We could make observations on facts like 'We're going to run out of water, what can we do?' as opposed to, 'There's not enough water, I knew we'd run out!' or 'I'd love some seasoning,' as opposed to 'This food has no taste!'

This made people realize how many times a day their comments would be complaints! The people on the trip corrected themselves, changed their tone, and when we thought it sounded like a complaint, we would laugh and ask them if it was a statement or a complaint.

For three weeks at least, there was no complaining, and the teams grew very close to each other. The positive environment made the work easier for all of us.

—SM

So, we told them the story from our trip to Kenya and how we addressed the complaining of our fellow travelers.

At the end of the story, we asked a simple question, 'How do you think reducing the complaining helped these teams?'

The team engaged in a discussion where they agreed about when and where complaining and emotive language would be out of bounds. The story allowed the team to be more honest about their own behaviors.

They agreed with their leader and amongst themselves, that they would make every effort to stop the complaining and start afresh. They discussed using more positive language and encouraging each other by providing regular feedback and reviewing the situation at their monthly meetings. The new leader was also able to focus on increasing their circles of influence.

So, let's look at some ideas to get you started using stories effectively:

Tell stories about your experiences as a team member. Perhaps an issue was resolved, or something memorable was said or done by a client that could be used as an example of a topic you want to discuss with the team.

My Grandma Told Me

Think also about stories your grandparents told you. People often tell us how much of an influence parents and family can have on things they have said or done, and older generations often have a wealth of stories that are still relevant today.

We provide a document that one of our grandmothers wrote nearly 90 years ago to give to her staff. What do you think about this advice? Would you add or change anything today? We have used this before to simply get a team talking. The story is both personal and one that could encourage an interesting exchange.

Cultural stories are often useful to make a point too. You can use idioms or stories from different cultures to express an idea. Remember in the last chapter the Kahlil Gibran quotation of the doves.

Once you've told the story, it then becomes a 'shortcut' that you can use to remind people when facing difficult situations.

GRANDMA'S
STAFF MANAGEMENT PRINCIPLES

Sufficient knowledge of one's own job is of great importance, and the capability of imparting this knowledge is also necessary.

Confidence in oneself and being able to do the work with confidence.

Must have a liking for people and one's fellow beings.

When dealing with one's staff, it is advisable to lead and not push and ask them to do something, not command.

A sense of humor is necessary, as it often prevents a difficult situation from getting out of hand.

Tell the staff the reason for making or changing the rules.

Remove the Ego from the Equation

When addressing a conflict, be sure that there is a real problem and that *you* are not just in a bad mood. Try to identify the real issues or opportunity, not just the symptoms or personalities. Remove your ego from the equation and be prepared to work toward winning.

Keep some perspective because relationships are not destroyed with conflict and can often be enhanced when you work toward a mutually satisfactory solution to conflict.

Look for a win-win and do your best to be empathic, put yourself in the others person's shoes.

Try to avoid thinking it's their problem, and own part of it if you are in conflict. If you are giving feedback about the issue describe it rather than judge it.

Be specific and establish a common goal and be persistent in coming to a satisfactory solution if it's important to you.

At the end of a discussion to resolve conflict, summarize what has been decided and who will take any next steps.

Never check any member of staff in front of the other unless it is unavoidable, and by doing so, an accident can be avoided.

Always give the correct information when a new member joins the team.

It is essential to have confidence in the staff and the staff to have confidence in the person in charge, and it is advisable to listen to genuine grievances but Do Not Listen to Tales.

Do not allow difficult situations to get out of hand; get expert advice when necessary and so avoid a difficult situation.

Written by my grandmother for her team leads in 1934.

—SM

A genuine desire to resolve conflict is a great asset.Having an overblown sense of self-importance, for example, thinking that a title will result in respect or authority, is a big barrier to effective leadership and teamwork. If you are too busy with your ego, it will be harder to care about others.

By improving your and your team's communication skills, you can all adapt and relate to people more effectively, contributing to your team's overall success.

Remember the Grapes

One such story, *Remember the Grapes*, comes from traditional village life in Lebanon. We tell this story to highlight the need to stay focused on the goals and not necessarily win an argument.

When someone gets stuck in an argument, we simply remind them with a simple statement: 'Remember the grapes'. It quickly gets them focused on the goals. It works every time!

We bet that there are many idioms in your culture or the culture of others that you can use!

Sometimes telling a story about a mistake you made can be funny and highlight a learning opportunity. We've often used the story of 'Falling Off a Horse' used in chapter 4 to show that it is OK to make mistakes—if you can learn from them.

You can make your interactions more varied and productive. Sometimes something as simple as saying, 'That reminds me of...' and then telling a relevant story can introduce a new perspective to a conversation.

So, make sure you choose the story to suit your point and use your storytelling skills to convey it.

THE GRAPES STORY

As you walk from one village to another in the mountains of Lebanon, passing through the vineyards, tradition says you can pick grapes and eat them on the way but not fill your pockets.

Now and again, you will bump into a guard who will question what you are doing.

As he questions you, be nice, and find a way to gain his trust.

Remember that you are there to **eat the grapes,** not fight with the guard. —YA

Be a role model.

Building trusting and mutually respectful relationships is important.

Connect, relate, and engage with others.

Don't underestimate the small talk. It matters to some people.

Embrace the diversity of the people you interact with.

Be open to sharing your thinking and reasoning to help others understand your conclusions.

Extend your sphere of influence to become more effective.

Remove your ego from the equation by being Adult and be careful not to bruise others' egos.

Use stories to impact how you coach and help others.

KEY IDEAS

CHAPTER

6

CLARIFYING AND SETTING THE DIRECTION

Leadership is the art of influencing and directing people to accomplish the mission. The basic concept the effective leader must keep in mind encompasses two fundamental elements: The mission, The people.

US AIR FORCE
AIR FORCE LEADERSHIP

The Role of a Leader

Your role as a leader is to set direction, identify priorities, clarify accountabilities, provide resources, build bridges, and remove obstacles so that your team can do what they do best. The leader's role is to

Explain the WHY
Define the WHAT
Assign the WHO

and

Leave the HOW to the team.

As a leader, you will be expected to get things done, but you won't be expected to do the work yourself.

You will be expected to clarify what needs to be done, ensure the team has the motivation, skills, tools, and resources needed to finish the work and remove any obstacles out of their way.

By staying out of the weeds and keeping the team focused on the big picture, you not only inspire your team to act but also free them up to come up with solutions that you may have never thought of.

Define Your Team's Mission

A good place to start is by defining your team's mission. Do that by asking yourself:

What is the raison d'être for your team?
What is my team supposed to accomplish?
How does what we do add value to our organization?
How do we keep our team relevant?
Why do we do what we do?
Why do we even exist?

'You are not paid to do. You are paid to be.'

UNKNOWN

LET HER BE!

CONTEXT
CRISIS
When Yahya joined the new organization, he took over from Xavier, who had been leading the technical team for a year.

During Yahya's first week on the job, as he was transitioning departmental priorities with Xavier, the network manager, Zora, walked in to let them know that the company network was down.

X'S APPROACH
Xavier quickly jumped in and, as team leader, started bombarding Zora with hard questions:

'What happened?

'Why did it happen?

'Who was doing what?

'When?'

STOP!

Y'S APPROACH
Yahya, on the other hand, addressed Zora with one simple question:

'Do you have what you need to get to the bottom of this?'

'Yes', Zora replied confidently, to which Yahya added,

'Please go take care of it, and keep me posted'.

Z'S SOLUTION
As Zora went to attend to the network, Xavier was feeling very uneasy. He didn't like being kept out of the details and even more anxious because he was unable to join Zora at the data center to 'help' with the debugging.

Noticing Xavier's discomfort, Yahya was trying to engage with him, looking after his concern. A few minutes later Zora strode in, stating flatly that the network problem had been solved.

ANALYSIS
DON'T DO. BE.
By Yahya–and Xavier— staying out of Zora's way, not only did her team solve the problem in record time, but they also felt empowered to come up with optimal solutions. In addition to solving the problem, Yahya also gained the trust of Zora that day, becoming one of his best performers.

Be like Yahya: Always let your team know you are there for them and, most importantly, know when to step out of their way—to empower them.

YOU NEED TO RESIST THE URGE TO 'DO'. JUST 'BE'.
–YA

For your mission to be effective, you must ensure you have the buy-in from the team and other stakeholders. For that, make sure that you involve them in drafting it.

So, start with sharing a draft with your own leader to make sure you are aligned. Let them know this is a draft and you are working with your team to refine it. Ask for feedback to ensure you align with your leadership's thinking and adjust accordingly.

Once you align with your own leader, hand over your draft of the mission statement to a group of motivated members on your team and ask them to discuss and refine it among themselves. Let them do that on their own without your interference and ask them to meet with you when they have an updated version.

Make sure to listen to their feedback and incorporate their recommendations while staying aligned with your manager.

Once you agree on the mission, have the group who helped you draft it to communicate it with the rest of your team. By asking them to present and discuss the mission, you gain even more buy-in and engagement from the team. This will, in turn, help team members who go on to lead to have an example of how this should work.

MISSION

SHMISSION BLA BLA BLA

In one global organization the authors both worked with, the new CEO developed a new but rather long mission statement with three or four paragraphs. He announced that everyone should know this mission and often stopped people in meetings or corridors to ask them to recite it back. One team was going to the USA for a meeting. One of the members was so afraid of being asked about the mission and getting it wrong that he wrote it on his shirt cuff and along the arm of the shirt in indelible ink. How can we expect people to be engaged when learning the statement is more important than aligning with it and living it in action?

–SM

Share Your Team's Mission

Don't forget to use every opportunity to share your team's mission with all your other stakeholders. Everyone must know what you and your team are trying to achieve.

Keep It Simple

As you work on the mission, make sure not to fall into the trap of an all-encompassing statement that is hard to remember.

We have seen many mission statements that are a page long. These mission statements are too complex and vague to be clear or actionable and too difficult to remember or internalize.

The best missions can be summarized in concise and crisp statements and are easy to remember 'to be lived by tag lines'.

Here are a couple of good examples of tag lines. An IT team supporting a world-class academic institution:

> **Our mission is to partner with academic units to transform teaching, research, and student life by developing and maintaining superior communications and computing infrastructure and providing prompt and knowledgeable support to all users of digital communications and computing.**

An IT team whose mission is to build and deliver reliable state-of-the-art IT services to their clients:

> **Our mission is to build:**
> **Cool stuff. Easy to use.**
> **Doesn't break.**

WORKSHEET 7.1

DEVELOPING YOUR
MISSION STATEMENT

G2L

Some questions to help you develop your mission statement.

What is the purpose of our organization?

What goals are we going to achieve?

How does my team's existence relate to the organization's overall purpose?

How do these goals support the organization's mission?

What is the scope of this team?

Are the goals measurable?

How can my team contribute to the organization's goals & objectives?

How will we know when we have achieved them?

YOU GET WHAT YOU MEASURE

One of the best-performing companies Alex worked for had five key goals for the whole company.

Everyone's bonus depended on meeting all five goals.

If the company met 80% of its goals, everyone got their bonus.

≥**80**%

If, however, the company accomplished less than 80% of the targets, then no one— not even the CEO—got any of their bonus.

<**80**%

Additionally, if the company met 90% of the targets, everyone got 150% of their bonus.

≥**90**%   **1.5**X

FIGURE 7.1

Progress against these goals was measured and reported to everyone at the company once a month.

They discussed how well they were doing and more importantly, how they could help each other to meet those goals.

Because there was a set of unified, measurable goals that were followed religiously, and because their income depended on it, people overachieved their targets every year, and everyone got 150% of their bonus.

Keep your goals SMART (Simple, Measurable, Achievable, Relevant, and Timely), measure them, make progress against them, make them transparent, and connect them to tangible outcomes and the growth of your team. —YA

You Get What You Measure

The next step is to set measurable objectives and metrics related to your mission.

Setting clear goals makes it easier for the team to focus on what is important and helps you define success and recognize it when you get there.

You can do that by setting **'SMART'**—goals that relate to your team's mission:

SPECIFIC
SIMPLE · SENSIBLE · SIGNIFICANT

MEASURABLE
MEANINGFUL · MOTIVATING

ACHIEVABLE
AGREED · ATTAINABLE

RELEVANT
REALISTIC · RESULTS-BASED

TIME-BOUND
TIME-LIMITED + SENSITIVE

Make sure to keep track of these goals and share your progress with the rest of the team regularly.

We have found that an optimal number of SMART goals should be in the range of 3–7. Too few goals make them too generic to be useful, while too many make them impossible to manage.

While some of the goals you set could be specific to individuals, having team-wide goals is important. By having shared team goals, you encourage everyone to work together to achieve your mission.

Your team's SMART goals will depend on the mission of your organization and team. As a new leader, taking the time to develop meaningful goals will help you drive success in a structured way.

ACRONYM ALERT!
SMART
SPECIFIC
MEASURABLE
ACHIEVABLE
RELEVANT
TIME-BOUND

DEVELOPING
SMART
G O A L S

A SMART approach to goals can help your team and you as a leader: focus your team's and your efforts, track progress, attain achievable aims, keep relevance and alignment to other goals, and have deadlines that you can work toward.

SMART goals are now **SMARTER**— The new **R** is for 'consistently **REVIEW** where you are'.

5
AVERAGE
SMART
G O A L S

TEN **SMART GOAL** SAMPLES

FIGURE 7.2

IN THE NEXT YEAR

RELIABILITY
99% AVAILABILITY OF ALL CRITICAL SYSTEMS

<1% OF SEVERITY 1 ISSUES

SUSTAINABILITY
-10% REDUCTION IN OPERATING COSTS

$100K TO RAISE IN EXTERNAL FUNDING

SCALABILITY
20% INCREASE IN USERS

-10% COST REDUCTION PER USER

SECURITY
0 DATA BREACHES

4HR RESPONSE TO SEVERITY 1 CASES

CUSTOMER EXPERIENCE
90% END-USER SATISFACTION

0 ESCALATIONS TO CIO

CAPACITY BUILDING
85% STAFF RETENTION

100% ITIL STAFF CERTIFICATE

INNOVATION
1 INTRODUCE ONE NEW PRODUCT

RELEVANCE
80% UTILIZATION OF ALL SERVICES

COMPLIANCE
100% CLEAN AUDIT REPORTS

0 GDPR VIOLATIONS

AGILITY
90% PROJECTS ON TIME

4HR RESOLUTION OF ALL CRITICAL ISSUES

FIGURE 7.3

SIX
CORE
VALUES

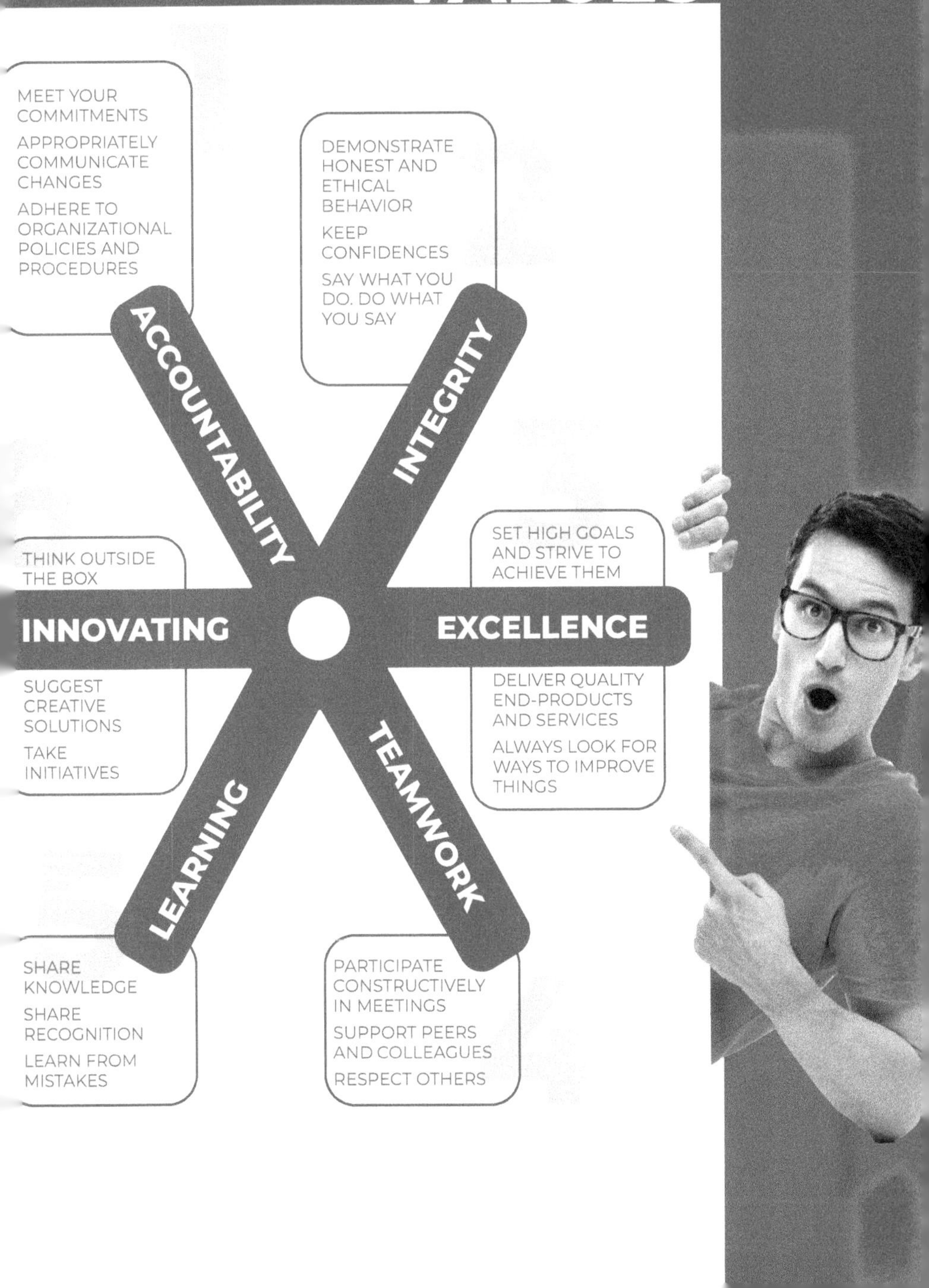

ACCOUNTABILITY

MEET YOUR COMMITMENTS

APPROPRIATELY COMMUNICATE CHANGES

ADHERE TO ORGANIZATIONAL POLICIES AND PROCEDURES

INTEGRITY

DEMONSTRATE HONEST AND ETHICAL BEHAVIOR

KEEP CONFIDENCES

SAY WHAT YOU DO. DO WHAT YOU SAY

INNOVATING

THINK OUTSIDE THE BOX

SUGGEST CREATIVE SOLUTIONS

TAKE INITIATIVES

EXCELLENCE

SET HIGH GOALS AND STRIVE TO ACHIEVE THEM

DELIVER QUALITY END-PRODUCTS AND SERVICES

ALWAYS LOOK FOR WAYS TO IMPROVE THINGS

LEARNING

SHARE KNOWLEDGE

SHARE RECOGNITION

LEARN FROM MISTAKES

TEAMWORK

PARTICIPATE CONSTRUCTIVELY IN MEETINGS

SUPPORT PEERS AND COLLEAGUES

RESPECT OTHERS

How You Do Things Is Also Important

In addition to setting goals, you also need to set expectations for your team's behavior.

These expectations, often referred to as **Core Values,** define the team's culture and are critical to the team's performance and how the rest of the organization perceives them.

Just like the mission and goals, getting buy-in from your team is key to developing and implementing your core values is invaluable.

But That Is Not Enough

To build a team culture, you need to ensure that your core values are not just 'fancy words'.

The core values need to translate to everyday observable behaviors that you can hold each other accountable against.

Start by articulating what is most important to you.

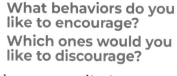

What behaviors do you like to encourage?
Which ones would you like to discourage?

Make sure your list is not too long.

Like the mission, you need to make sure that you have buy-in from the team. So, once you have a list in mind, get a small group on your team to refine it.

144

Ask them to consolidate this list to no more than a 'handful' of important values. Also, ask them to define these values by associating expected behaviors with each.

These behaviors should be something that team members can recognize and hold each other accountable for. You may have to support them in this too!

Clarify Roles and Responsibilities

One cause of conflict and stress on teams is the lack of clarity around roles and responsibilities. When roles are unclear, people will end up stepping on each other's toes or, worse, dropping the ball on critical services and deliverables.

Although organization structures help clarify roles, many projects and services depend on the collaboration between multiple individuals across different groups to get things done. This normally blurs any predefined responsibility lines, offering opportunities for some people to take advantage of it.

LOOK AT WHAT I DID!

One of the first things the new leader wanted to do was run sessions with all the staff to work on a new vision and mission statement. He gathered all the suggestions, ran a smaller session to test the draft, and asked staff to make any amendments. The statement, including its development process, was presented to the entire staff at a town hall meeting. Sandy was sitting in the auditorium and happened to overhear a conversation that she can still clearly recall. The young woman sitting beside her turned to her colleagues and said, 'See the 'and must' in line 3? I was in the meeting that changed that line. I put that in.' When people feel they are a part of something, it can inspire and motivate them. Inclusion is a powerful way to feel valued.
—SM

Overly ambitious staff may take advantage of this ambiguity and overstep their bounds to look like heroes, while other 'survivors' will take this opportunity to avoid decision-making and pass the blame onto others. Both types of behavior lead to stress, conflict, and, most importantly, delivery issues.

A big part of clarifying roles is explicitly assigning an owner for each task, project, or service to resolve any role ambiguity.

Do not assign ownership to a group, team, or title. Instead, make sure you assign ownership to a person by name.

Although the owner is

SAMPLE
RACI
MATRIX

Here is an oversimplified example of a RACI matrix for a small bakery.

FIGURE 7.4

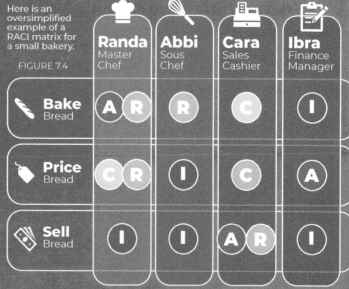

	Randa Master Chef	**Abbi** Sous Chef	**Cara** Sales Cashier	**Ibra** Finance Manager
Bake Bread	A R	R	C	I
Price Bread	C R	I	C	A
Sell Bread	I	I	A R	I

Randa is accountable for ensuring that the correct number and type of goodies are baked. She needs to consult with Cara on what and how much to bake, as Cara knows what is being sold. Once agreed, Randa and Abbi start baking and keeping Ibra in the loop on what they baked. Ibra is accountable for setting the pricing on the goodies. However, to do that, he needs to understand what it takes to bake and how much people are willing to pay for gourmet bread. For that, he consults with Randa

and Abbi. Cara is the one who is accountable for ensuring that all the breads are sold. Since there is no one else in the front of the store, she is the one who does the actual selling as well.

NOTE
The columns are listed by the person's name in addition to their role. By assigning a name, you clarify accountability. Each row has only one person accountable (only one A). Some cells have multiple letters like AR). Some rows have multiples of the same role.

accountable for ensuring things get done, they don't have to do all the work themselves.

By explicitly assigning a task to a person, you simultaneously clarify where the accountability is and empower that person to lead.

Make a RACI Matrix

For more complex projects involving larger teams, defining a matrix using a **RACI** structure helps:

RESPONSIBLE
ACCOUNTABLE
CONSULT
INFORM

A RACI matrix maps the people with their tasks. Essentially, it is a table whose columns are the names of the resources working on the project, while the rows define their tasks. Each resource is then assigned one of the following roles:

ACCOUNTABLE
This is the 'owner' of the task, and they are ultimately **accountable** for ensuring that the task is accomplished. Every r ow should have one—and only one—accountable resource.

RESPONSIBLE
These are the people who are **responsible** for accomplishing the task. This could be one or more members from the same or different groups.

CONSULT
These resources need to be **consulted** before any decisions are made that could impact the scope or delivery of the work.

INFORM
These team members just need to 'be in the loop'. Informing them of progress and issues helps the project stay on track.

EMBRACING
POWER

MARSHA L. CLARK

' *To delegate is to commit or entrust to another. Delegation is a tool for developing others, giving them an opportunity to gain knowledge and perspective, planning and follow through skills and the importance of communication and accountability."*

MARSHA L CLARK

147

Learn to Say 'No'

Use your mission and goals to keep you and the team focused on what is important.

More important than being service-oriented is learning when and how to say no to requests not tied to your team's mission or goals.

'*What you permit, you promote*'

UNKNOWN

By accepting tasks not aligned with your mission and goals, you risk overloading your team with irrelevant work and, importantly, confusing the rest of your stakeholders about your team's roles and responsibilities.

Of course, an organization's priorities change over time.

You must constantly evaluate your mission and goals to ensure you and your team are aligned with the organization's priorities and that all stakeholders are aware of your roles.

It is also important to make sure that you call out those

who do not exhibit the core values your team espouses. By ignoring 'bad behavior,' you tacitly accept it and encourage others to do the same.

As important as it is to reward good behavior, it is even more important to let people who do not behave appropriately know that what they did, or how they did it, is unacceptable and what your expectations are. You then have an opportunity to help them develop different behaviors.

This message must be done clearly, professionally, and privately. The team members should know that you are trustworthy and that you have their interests at heart.

Three Leadership Tips

Your job as a leader is to ensure that the team lives and breathes the mission, goals, and core values, as this is what keeps the team focused and motivated and is the basis on which your team culture develops.

'Don't trample on my parsley patch.'

LEBANESE PROVERB

1 SCHEDULE REGULAR MEETINGS

To help you do that, schedule regular team meetings to review progress against goals. Remember to keep the objective of these meetings clear and run them with structure and timeliness, as we have suggested in an earlier chapter.

You can use these meetings to review your team's progress against your mission and goals and celebrate successes.

Use these meetings to highlight areas that need attention and ask your team for suggestions on addressing challenges.

The team's input is critical, as they can provide insights and solutions you missed, and you can get their buy-in for moving forward.

These meetings are also a good time to discuss the team's progress with respect to the agreed-upon core values.

2 MEASURE YOUR PROGRESS

Some teams measure how they are doing concerning core values by conducting regular surveys before the meeting. The results are shared at the team meeting, followed by a discussion on the best ways to encourage living these values.

Try to vary how you get this feedback, as people can get survey blind and pay less attention to detail.

One team we worked with achieved this by making a Vox pop video of people talking about the values and naming people in various teams that they felt had lived the values and the impact it had made. It was genuine and, in some parts, funny, so it revitalized the values and engaged everyone.

3 RECOGNIZE TEAM MEMBERS

In addition to regular meetings, you can find informal ways to recognize individuals for their contributions or exemplary behavior.

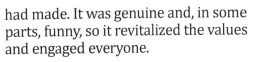

One approach is to create 'thank you cards' for each core value. These can be distributed by any team member to anyone they believe has demonstrated core value behaviors.

Most importantly, if you can tie the goals and core values into the performance review process, this is a reinforcement.

People will do what it takes to maximize the gains, and by tying your team's mission, goals, and core values to performance management, you encourage your team to focus on what is important.

Make sure that your performance review template addresses the behaviors linked to the core values and the contributions to team and individual goals.

It is a good idea to encourage the team members to self-assess those items and then discuss them with you, their leader, during the meeting.

Tying it All Together

So, put simply, your role as a leader is to clarify direction, provide the tools, and remove obstacles.

You need to consider that the mission defines your team's reason for being, and the goals define what your team should accomplish.

Once you get this established, you can develop some core values that will help you define how your team should behave. Putting together a RACI will help you to determine and manage accountability.

Ensuring all these are visible, well communicated, and tied to performance management ensures that your team stays focused on what is important.

Now you have some ideas about setting direction and getting clarity, we will look at teamwork.

Lead the way by providing direction and clarity.

Determine your team's mission.

Develop concise memorable statements and develop concise meaningful goals.

Create expectations of how the team needs to behave to build a strong collaborative culture.

Share core values.

Engage the team in all these activities.

Establish accountabilities and clarify roles to avoid ambiguities.

Focusing on these areas will help keep the team aligned to priorities.

This makes it easier to say 'No' to things that prevent the team from achieving their mission.

KEY IDEAS

CHAPTER

7

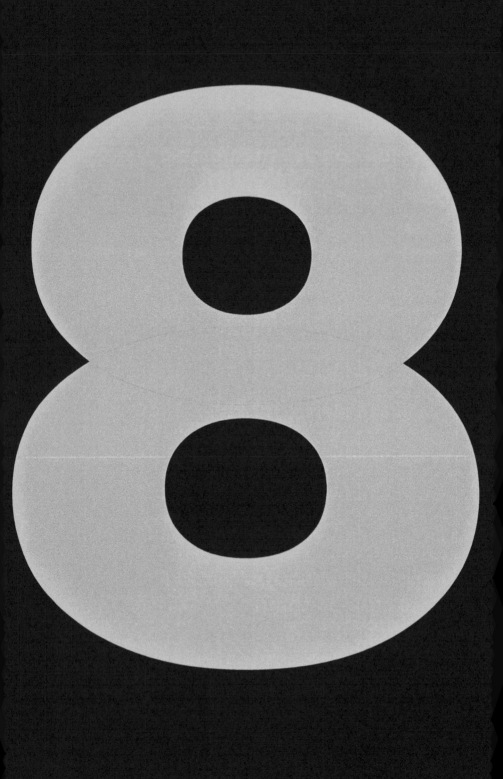

BUILDING THE TEAM

Given the relationship between teamwork and crucial business outcomes such as productivity, profitability, and customer perceptions of service quality... teams hold the keys to organizational health.

Building the Team

It is highly likely that before you take on your first leadership role, you will have been part of a team.

Hopefully, you will have experienced the positives of good teamwork and have learned lessons.

Regardless of your past experiences, you can start anew with your new team. In the following two chapters, we will be looking at what can help you start building and developing your team.

Undeniably, a team can accomplish more than one individual. However, not all teams are cohesive, which can create difficulties in delivery and performance, as well as strained relationships among team members.

As a leader, if you devote time to creating a healthy team, building the core values and desired behaviors together with the team, you can begin to create a stronger team.

Teams Are Dynamic

A team is not set in stone; it is dynamic and will change over time.

People may join or leave the team, and each time this occurs, you need to readjust the dynamics of the team. As a team leader it will make life more enjoyable if you can consistently build the healthiest team.

Without a strong foundation, a team can quickly become unproductive, despite appearing to be busy (which can be mistaken for being productive if there are no clear goals in place). They may be uncertain of their direction, and positive relationships may suffer as a result.

To build a solid base for your team, we recommend that you start by considering how you can build trust between the members and yourself.

Trust is the foundation

The foundation of the team must be built on trust. It is the most important quality and characteristic. Being trustworthy involves two key elements: character and competence. People need to be able to trust your intentions and your capabilities. As a leader, you must be trustworthy and not waste time and energy trying to look good or engaging in political games. Establish your own personal credibility.

'He who does not trust enough, will not be trusted.'

LAO TZU

158

Keys to a Successful Team

Building a healthy team and being recognized as a trustworthy leader is a good start to creating a successful team.

As a new leader, you may feel anxious about the team getting the work done, so begin by making sure you know what skills you have in the team, effectively communicate clear expectations, and show your people you care.

You need to be visible, plan, monitor, be consistent and empower the team with the coaching skills you can put into practice every day. Trusting the team can also help the team members to feel more empowered and confident. Demonstrate that you value your team and are committed to their success.

Not everyone is easy to work with, but it is worthwhile to aim for a positive relationship with them.

'The ability to establish, grow, extend, and restore trust is the key professional and personal competency of our time.'

STEPHEN COVEY

Creating a healthier team

Identify and discuss individual strengths and how these strengths can contribute to the team's success. Share information freely and honestly, and authentical-ly. (Remember to be yourself with more skills).

Spend time planning the face-to-face meetings and working sessions with your team. Be available and present.

BUILDING TRUST

HERE ARE SOME BEHAVIORS THAT WILL HELP TO BUILD TRUST.

Learn to trust others and show your own trustworthiness.

Getting your team to really open themselves up and trust each other is a good start but **take your time.** Remember that people may have worked together for a long time, but this doesn't necessarily mean they trust each other. You need to build and maintain trust continuously.

It may be uncomfortable at first for people to **exhibit vulnerability,** but they will once they trust you and each other.

Don't **shy away from crucial conversations,** be clear and specific. Be honest.

Listen to people and then you can work to be understood. Be attentive and present with others.

Even if it causes more issues, **it's better to be real.** Don't bury your head in the sand. Make sure you check the 'reality' in terms of your thinking and how your personal interpretations or subjective information may impact you and others. (Recall the Ladder of Inference?)

Show respect by acknowledging people are doing the best they can in the world in which they operate and offer coaching to help them develop.

Openly share information but balance that with the need to know and confidentiality.

Don't leave things that are not working even if this results in some people being unhappy.

Try not to be drawn into gossip or talking about others. When team members hear you engaging in these types of interaction, it becomes more difficult to trust you.

Defend your people publicly. Know your team well enough to defend them, but also be able to give honest feedback.

Assure you **align the results to the mission and goals** you have created as a team. Consider what outcomes you are looking for and how you expect your team to get there. Pay attention to the results and track progress.

Own what you are responsible for and encourage the team to be accountable.

Check your team is **not over promising** and encourage them to say no when activities are not supporting the objectives.

Deliver on your commitments to increase credibility and reliability.

Always look to improve. Become agile at learning and stay curious.

Take time to self-monitor and solicit feedback on your actions and behaviors from the team and others you trust.

Trust, however, is not a given, it must be earned. Discuss the importance of trust in your team and provide examples of when people have proven trustworthy. When you put your trust in someone to deliver on their promises and keep them, make sure it is acknowledged. Make sure you honor your own commitments.

You can help strengthen the team's trust by establishing common ground rules for engaging in conflict. Ensure the team is respectful and address issues with care and attention, and encourage them to feel comfortable disagreeing, without being personal.

Conflict is necessary for productive meetings because it can uncover and build upon other's ideas, spark creativity, and introduce alternatives. If you understand the natural conflict style of each member and provide feedback and coaching, you will be helping to develop their skills.

Tensions in relationships are often due to unresolved conflict and the team needs to trust that it is safe to engage in healthy conflict.

Gaining Commitment

When the team trust you and each other they can then start to focus more on alignment, understanding what needs to be done, by whom, and when. The collaboration increases. Be sure to review and monitor commitments regularly.

Adopt a 'disagree and commit' mentality—encourage the team members to commit regardless of initial disagreements. Make definitive statements such as, 'So, this is what we have agreed!' Get people to acknowledge the

'The day soldiers stop bringing you their problems is the day you have stopped leading them. They have either lost confidence that you can help them or concluded that you do not care. Either case is a failure of leadership.'

COLIN POWELL

161

commitments made, make sure people feel they have been heard but remind them that silence signifies consent.

Being Accountable

When you are discussing goals and activities, make it clear who is accountable for what and by when. Address issues where people are not being accountable, rather than ignoring them, but also take the time to understand why issues may be occurring.

It is also important to address poor performance within the team, otherwise team members who are performing well will feel demotivated, and the team will become dysfunctional. Regular feedback on how accountable the team members are is key.

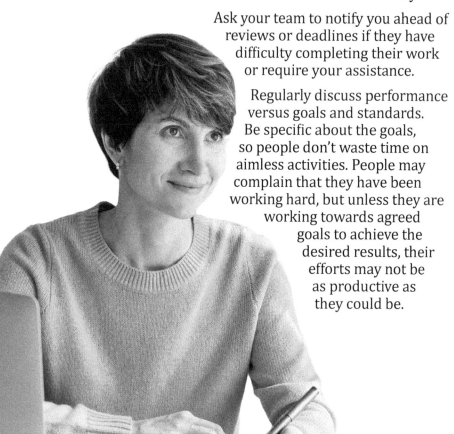

Ask your team to notify you ahead of reviews or deadlines if they have difficulty completing their work or require your assistance.

Regularly discuss performance versus goals and standards. Be specific about the goals, so people don't waste time on aimless activities. People may complain that they have been working hard, but unless they are working towards agreed goals to achieve the desired results, their efforts may not be as productive as they could be.

HEALTHY VS UNHEALTHY TEAMS

AN **UNHEALTHY TEAM** MAY EXHIBIT SOME OF THE FOLLOWING BEHAVIORS

Team members may insist that everything is fine and **fail to flag bad news.**

The team **doesn't share information** or knowledge, resulting in duplicated efforts.

The **leader serves as the only conduit** for conversations, which can prevent the team from resolving issues or working well together.

Poor time management may make the team seem busy, but they may not be as productive as they could be.

Autonomy is sometimes mistaken for accountability. Technical people can often enjoy working on their own, but the desire for autonomy must be aligned with accountability. They are still a part of shared goals.

The team may appear to be firefighting to fix issues (techies love to fix things), but they need to be mindful that they are not just **fixing the problems they created in the first place.**

The team may **not be resolving conflicts** and instead may choose to avoid working with certain members altogether.

Team members may feel a **lack of purpose** and may not see the bigger picture.

A **HEALTHY TEAM** IS ONE IN WHICH THE TEAM IS

Clear about the team's **purpose**, scope, and role in it.

Clear about the **goals** they are striving for and what is expected of them.

Clear about how their team's work fits into the **bigger pictur**e of the organization.

Able to discuss things **openly** and challenge each other.

Meet regularly, are **transparent**, and share information, including with their leader.

Align on team **values** and working practices and agreed standards and processes.

Allow time for regular **feedback**.

Provide opportunities for personal **growth** and development.

Trustworthy as a group and as individuals.

Collaborative. The team needs to discuss what this means to them so that the word is not just organizational jargon but tangible to them.

—SM

Focus on Results

Encourage the team to focus on the results. Keep them focused on tangible group goals. Review objectives, goals, and their progress frequently. Determine the desired results and review the impact of them when the goals have been reached. Develop a mindset that consistently seeks to achieve the objectives that have been set and agreed upon.

Reward individuals for their achievement of team objectives and the success of the group.

Technical people can often get carried away with the technology and overcomplicate their solutions, so keep the focus on what the team needs to achieve.

A team that addresses and focuses on these positive elements will perform better. It can feel daunting for a new leader to manage performance, but your relationships with the team will be key to the team achieving results consistently.

FIRST TALE ON TRANSPARENCY

Mark was leading a team of nine people. It was his first leadership role. He received his first 360 feedback assessment and was upset by the results, particularly the low score in the trust category. On further investigation, the team explained that Mark often kept things from them that they later heard about from other teams.

When Mark heard this, he was confused as he felt he was shielding the team from negative news. **He learned that there are certain things that the team may need to know, even if it is bad news,** so that they can work through difficulties together and build trust in their leader.

–SM

MORAL 1 SHARE THE BAD NEWS!

164

Acknowledge Good Work

In *Whale Done!*, a book he coauthored with animal trainers, Ken Blanchard discusses the parallels that can be made from watching how the trainers achieved great results. Their success was based on four factors:

Building trust.

Accentuating the positive.

Redirecting energy away from negative or destructive energy.

Catching them doing the right things.

Be Transparent

Successful company leaders know the key to good leadership is transparency: Trust increases exponentially when you tell the truth as it is. Transparency involves keeping your team well informed and sharing the good as well as the bad with them. If the team can give you and each other feedback openly and resolve conflicts, plus overcome the discomfort of feeling vulnerable, you can develop more trusting and honest relationships.

SECOND TALE ON TRANSPARENCY

Roberta was new to leadership and was asked to reorganize the team in response to the pandemic. She met with her team frequently and was as open as possible.

The reorganization involved downsizing, and Roberta was honest about this with the team.

It was a difficult period for the team, but they thanked Roberta for her transparency and trusted that she was doing her best for them.
—SM

MORAL 2 BE HONEST

Ensure that your team feels supported and can approach you with their concerns, trusting that you will have their back and act in their best interests as well as those of the team.

There will be times when you may need to prioritize the well-being of the business or organization. But you can continue to treat your people with respect. If you've earned their trust, they will recognize that you're being as transparent as you are able, and doing the best you can under the circumstances.

Vulnerability Based Trust

In his work on teams in *The Five Dysfunctions of a Team*, Patrick Lencioni focuses on the concept of vulnerability-based trust. He suggests that for team members to truly trust one another, they must become accustomed to being open and honest about the challenges and their shortcomings, in other words, they must become more 'vulnerable.'

Being able to say things like

'I'm wrong.'

'I've made a mistake here.'

'I don't know enough yet.'

'Mary is better at this than the rest of us.'

'John came up with an idea I hadn't even thought of!'

'I'm stuck.'

will save time and energy over thinking about what to say or what will make you look better.

Developing vulnerability-based trust requires courage. If the leader exhibits this behavior, the team can be encouraged to behave in the same way.

It's about not being afraid to apologize if you've made a mistake or believe your behavior was inappropriate, such as losing your temper or expressing your frustration with someone. Remember that you are only human, even if you are working hard on managing emotions and reactive behavior.

An authentic apology, which evidences some personal reflection, can be an effective way to correct a mistake and help restore the trust required to keep a good relationship going. But remember, an apology without a change in behavior is not enough.

We mentioned earlier about acknowledging people, and it is also important to give attribution to the sources of your information or new ideas. People learn to trust you if they know you have the humility to acknowledge their input to your leadership abilities and knowledge. You will learn from your team.

One-on-One Meetings

Another way that you can build trust is to have One-on-Ones with each of your team members on a regular basis.

Relate, connect, and engage with your team. To do this, it's important to make time for each of your team members. A good way to do this is to schedule time in your calendar.

> *'Don't be afraid to show your vulnerability. Be transparent with your team, even when the truth may be unpopular or inconvenient.'*
>
> BILL GEORGE

Businesses are busy places, and time can fly by, so try to have a meeting at least once a month. Some leaders we have worked with schedule it more frequently, but the environment in which you work may dictate how frequently you meet.

This is not a meeting for status updates or the general exchange of organizational information; this can be done in a larger team meeting or meetings where the team discusses goals and core values.

This is an opportunity to get to know your team members and connect with them, learning about their likes and dislikes, challenges, and successes.

Here are some questions that might help you get started. These questions may initially feel strange, but you will develop your own style with each team member the more you practice.

'So, how's it all going?'

You will have an opportunity to provide feedback in this session. So, note things that are positive and things that might require more constructive feedback. You may also hear feedback about the team member, the team, or other. If they reply with 'OK,' ask:

'Tell me more about OK?'

'What does OK look like to you?

'What's on your mind right now?'

They may have something on their mind that's keeping them from focusing on this meeting. If they share their concern with you, you can decide whether to address it immediately, set it aside until later, or plan for another meeting, depending on the nature of the issue.

You may not need all of these but having them on hand and being able to use a variety of them in different meetings, is a good start.

Choose some you feel comfortable asking, but don't overload the conversation with too many questions. You can reword them to suit your style but keep to the essence of the questions and enjoy the conversation.

GOOD TIPS FOR A GOOD
One-on-One

'How was your week on a personal level?'

'Can you think of a small victory you had this week?'

'Did you face any roadblocks this week?'

'Do you have any pending questions I didn't answer during the week?'

'What progress do you feel you have made since our last session?'

'What actions have you taken? Are there any that you have not taken yet? What do you think prevented you from completing those?'

'Is there anything you feel hasn't worked for you since our last session?'

'What sort of issues did you face this week (or since we last chatted)? Did you overcome them?

If so, how? If not, what do you think you might do to go forward? Is there anything others or I can do to help?'

'What are the top three achievements you've made since our last session?'

'What could have gone better in the time we've had between sessions? What result are you trying to achieve?'

'What would be the most helpful thing for you to take away today?'

'Do you need any technical help from me this week?'

'Finally, let's agree on the next steps and actions before we meet next time.'

You can ask them meaningful questions that get them thinking and enable you to do some coaching as part of these exchanges. Take notes in these meetings. It will help you track progress and pick up on details. Involve the team members in the preparation of your meetings by asking them to suggest agenda items they would like to address in their One-on-One with you.

Focus on Accomplishments Rather than on Tasks

These meetings also allow you to learn more about the team because issues or conflicts can be viewed from various perspectives. As you build trust, you can give more constructive feedback and use your coaching competency.

Ensure that you are present in these sessions and not texting or emailing. That can be counterproductive and make people feel less valued. You are aiming to make a real connection.

Stay on Schedule

It is also important to keep these meetings on schedule. Rescheduling for something you see as a higher priority can often demotivate people and make them feel less important and defeats the purpose of the One-on-One.

You and the team member will recognize a true business emergency, but when these occur, try to reschedule as close to the initial meeting as possible.

170

These are crucial meetings for you and your team to connect and engage with each other more meaningfully than in your day-to-day communications. You will achieve better results if you plan for these meetings.

These One-on-Ones can provide a framework for both non-technical and technical leaders who are new to their leadership roles, as well as begin to reinforce credibility and show concern for the teams.

Be Attentive

Make sure you are attentive and listening. Outline the purpose for a One-on-One. Set the context for the meetings.

For example,

'So first, this is a meeting about you.

What we will do in these meetings is discuss you, your work, how you can progress, and what I can do to help you move forward.

It's a great opportunity to catch up as we get so busy during our day-to-day activities. How does that sound?'

Whether the initial response is negative, neutral, or positive, just get going with the same positive approach.

Note what you agree upon to pick up where you left off.

As your confidence grows, you will follow your team members' lead and focus on your relationships with them. This approach will eventually become more prominent in your leadership style.

The foundation of a healthy team is trust.

As a leader you need to be trustworthy.

Be as transparent as you can and develop vulnerability-based trust in the team.

Make time for the team members and meet with them One-on-One regularly.

Build the components of a healthy team and expect each team member to play their part.

You cannot rush intimacy but be consistent.

Be honest.

Accentuate the positive. Keep the team's energy positive.

Catch people doing the right things.

KEY IDEAS

CHAPTER

8

DEVELOPING YOUR TEAM MEMBERS

Before you are a leader, success is all about growing yourself. When you become a leader, success is all about growing others.

JACK WELCH

Develop Others

Your self-development as a leader will be an ongoing process, but one of your most rewarding leadership activities will be developing others.

Helping your team members with their personal and career growth can increase their employment prospects, boost their confidence, and lead to a more motivated and productive workforce.

Developing a strategy for your team's growth will also play an important part in helping them get where they want to go.

You will need to challenge them, provide support, and work together with them on their development to create opportunities for growth, promotions, or changes in direction. Also, you can help them to push themselves, while encouraging them to stay grounded, and develop an awareness of their abilities.

Technical people often enjoy being the best at what they do and strive for perfection which can be costly to them, their end users, and the business. Some want to take on more than they are capable of, too soon, and some may be happy doing just what is required, without a stretch.

'CFO:
What happens if we invest in developing our people and then they leave?

CEO:
What happens if we don't, and they stay!'

HENRY FORD

Others will want to take advantage of every opportunity and are driven to grow. You will face a range of development needs in your teams, and this can be both challenging and satisfying.

There are also a range of resources available to you such as: coaching on the job, mentoring, on-the-job training, knowledge sharing, conferences, seminars, secondments, job exchanges, and formal courses and accreditations.

Understand Each Other

Your one-on-one meetings with your team are also an excellent opportunity to discuss, not only their day-to-day accomplishments, but activities that can contribute to their in-dividual development plans. You can help them to work on the skills they use and need to develop, con-sider their challenges, and support them as they take the steps required to enhance their roles and them-selves. You will also learn to recognize opportunities to coach your team. Make sure the team know that you are available for

sistance between ses-
ons. They will appreci-
e this as you take op-
ortunities to coach them
 real time in your daily
teractions with them.

is, however, a
rtnership because
ey are also accountable
 work toward their
als and aspirations,
hich can build a
al connection
etween you. So, it's
nportant to make
 clear to the team
embers that they
e also responsible
r their own growth
d development.

ou will need to un-
erstand where each
 your team members
, regarding their skills,
rengths, challenges,
d aspirations. You
eed an understanding
 what they are think-
g about their roles and
eir futures.

his may take some time
 you have only recently
et the team. However,
ngage with them early
n to get their self-assess-
ents until you can make
ur own assessments.

A Relationship Contract

Here is an example of a working contract
drawn up by a team from a large IT
company. The team held each other
accountable for these behaviors and felt
it had helped develop them into a more
cohesive, healthier team.

Purpose
To challenge and support each other,
striving to deliver significant value in all
that we do. —SM

GUIDING PRINCIPLES

In working together, we:

Do what we say.

Are present and honest, always
setting and managing clear
expectations.

Question and challenge for
deeper understanding.

Acknowledge that successful
outcomes are a given!

Always look to the
'right' enablers.

Use our distinct strengths and
strive to go beyond.

Exchange and collaborate
openly on ideas, issues,
and tools.

Are purposeful and ever
conscious of the 'bigger picture'.

Seek out and provide valuable
feedback and respond to it
promptly and constructively.

Think 'value and outcome',
not just cost!

Believe and exhibit behavior
that is supportive and uplifting.

Share humor and have
fun together.

Manage Expectations

Managing expectations is also essential. So, unless you have the budget or resources, (and you may have to defend your training requirements budget), don't promise anything like training or attendance at courses/conferences unless you can guarantee this.

We have heard team members complain that some team members get more than they do. To address this, less experienced leaders may be tempted to provide training as a gift to address the perception of unfairness, rather than focusing on the fact that it is highly personal. The acquisition of skills or knowledge should be linked to the requirements of the job and the individual's development.

Your teams will have specific individual and team business goals that you will have worked on together. When individuals want to develop personal development goals, they can work on these with you.

We have worked in some organizations where people are encouraged to have these discussions but do not have to have specific goals for personal development or put anything in writing. However, we would recommend that you do try to help your teams to plan, and build on, their leadership and personal growth competencies.

If the team trusts each other and exhibits vulnerability-based trust you may also be able to encourage them to discuss some of their goals

'There are three essentials to leadership: humility, clarity and courage.'

CHAN
MASTER
FUCHAN
YUAN

with each other, encouraging their support of one another and increasing accountability to achieve team goals.

Be aware of your own knowledge and skills, and don't let your own limitations stifle the development of others. If you develop your teams effectively some may outgrow your skills as they navigate through their careers.

If you have team members who have the potential to be promoted, or take on a leadership role, make sure you invest in them. We have seen some leaders hold on to their best performers as they are valuable to the team, and they don't want to disrupt the team's balance. However, you must let them go. This is why succession planning is important.

The Personal Development Plan

When people work in busy environments where it is easy to lose track of the day's tasks, having a written plan and process in place can be extremely helpful in ensuring they keep focused on their own development activities.

A useful tool to add to your leadership toolbox is the Personal Development Plan (PDP).

Saying things like, 'I'll do that in the future', or 'I'll work on that in the next few weeks' can easily be misplaced by other activities, and there is little structure to that thinking: it's just that, thinking. It needs to be

ACRONYM
ALERT!

PDP

PERSONAL
DEVELOPMENT
PLAN

documented and tracked. *Res non verba,* actions not words.

The plan and documentation should become a working document that is realistic and relevant. If you work on this with the team members along with the appropriate support, coaching, mentoring, and formal training, you should be able to make learning a key part of the team's culture. Being clear is key, as people cannot develop what they cannot measure.

Putting an action plan together with a team member and discussing it on a regular basis greatly helps the performance review process. It can make annual reviews less of a task, make them feel like a familiar discussion, a natural closure of a year's work, and encourage the team members to feel more comfortable with the overall process.

Not all your team members will have lofty goals, so having each member have their own plan can help them progress in areas they want to grow in. Others may want more from their careers and, equally, would benefit from your support. To encourage ownership, ask team members to:

THINK ABOUT THEIR FUTURE ASPIRATIONS AND CAREER GOALS

Where do they think they would like to be/do?

What do they enjoy doing?

Do they feel passionate about any area of their current role that they could progress?

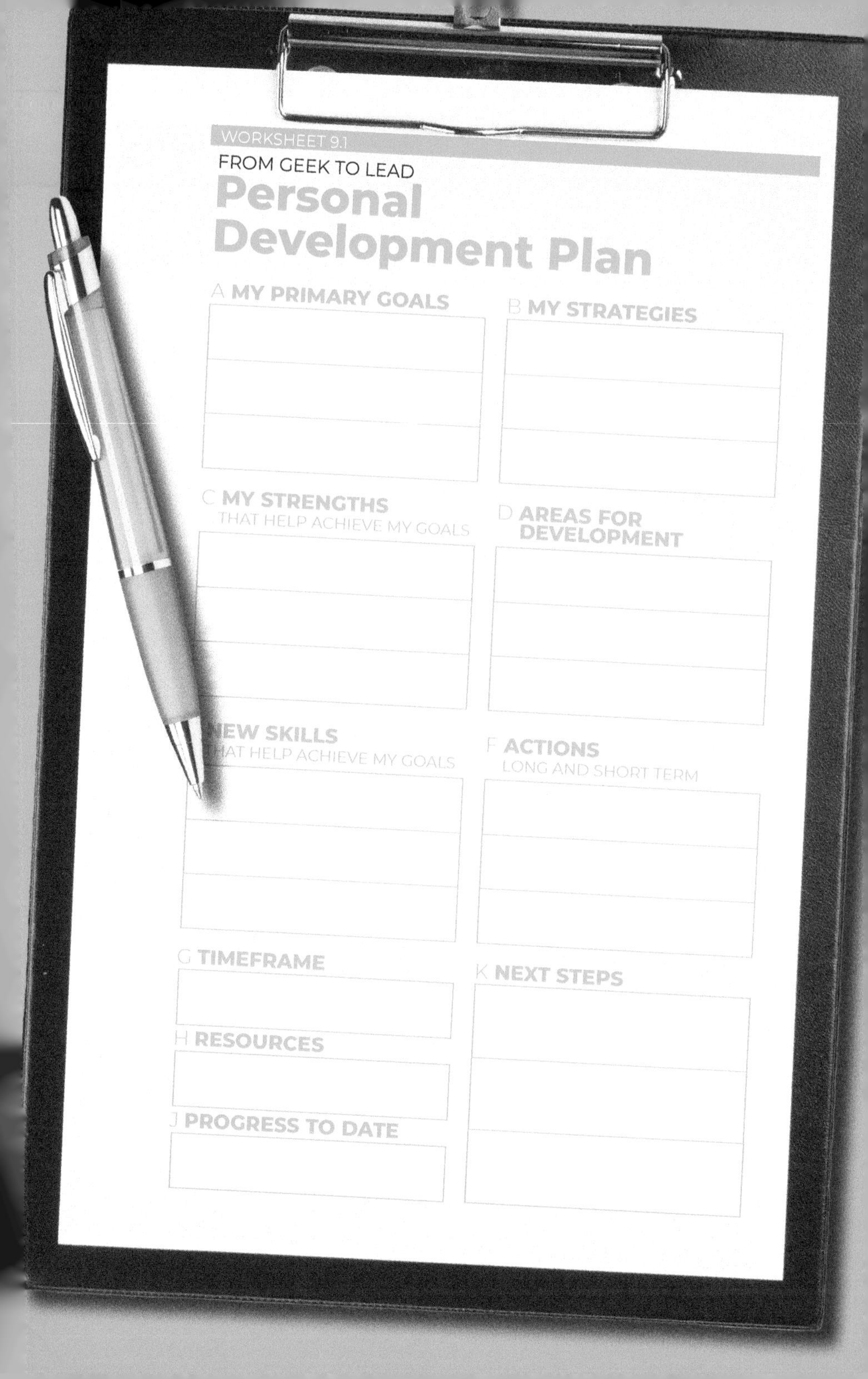

WORKSHEET 9.1

FROM GEEK TO LEAD

Personal Development Plan

A **MY PRIMARY GOALS**

B **MY STRATEGIES**

C **MY STRENGTHS**
THAT HELP ACHIEVE MY GOALS

D **AREAS FOR DEVELOPMENT**

NEW SKILLS
HAT HELP ACHIEVE MY GOALS

F **ACTIONS**
LONG AND SHORT TERM

G **TIMEFRAME**

H **RESOURCES**

J **PROGRESS TO DATE**

K **NEXT STEPS**

THINK ABOUT AND IDENTIFY THEIR STRENGTHS

Where do they feel most competent?

Can they identify five strengths?

THINK ABOUT THE AREAS THAT
THEY FEEL THEY NEED TO DEVELOP

Where do they need more knowledge, or have less gaps in.

Are there areas they would like to learn more about?

IDENTIFY THE PROGRESS THEY
BELIEVE THEY ARE MAKING

Can they provide examples?

What makes them feel this is progress? What do they feel are the areas in which they have made significant improvements?

THINK ABOUT WHAT THEY BELIEVE YOU AND THE
ORGANIZATION COULD DO TO HELP THEM.

Are You Still a Friend?

We have worked with new leaders who were concerned about their ability to remain friends with team members while also supporting them in a more formal capacity.

Your interactions around the team members' performance and development will be different from the previous ones you may have had as a peer, but both parties can benefit immensely from a process that engages them and has a structure.

If the team member feels uncomfortable with this at first, don't push. Help where you can and come back to it. It may take them time to adjust to a different relationship.

Create an Open Environment

Giving constructive and honest feedback is important too, as well as creating a positive and open environment to talk about issues. If you can do this and address the more contentious issues that often come up, the team will feel more comfortable about actively seeking feedback. Have regular meetings to monitor progress and celebrate successes.

Get close enough to see the issues, then step back to manage performance. You have a duty of care to all your team members, whether you have a friendship, or professional relationship.

Using skillful communication and processes that you can work on together with your team members can help them to recognize your leadership.

You may not have had these discussions with your colleagues if you were part of the team, but you can approach the personal development process with kindness and consideration. You may of course have a friendship, but it shouldn't prevent you from making tough decisions or giving feedback when it is needed. If you are professional, your attention to their growth and development could strengthen your relationship. Helping your team members grow and develop can be fulfilling and rewarding.

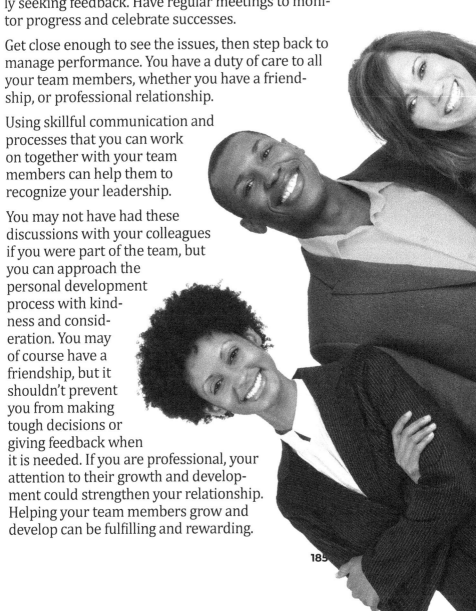

185

Give Constructive and Honest Feedback

Some leaders find it difficult to give feedback, and some team members find it difficult to solicit or receive constructive feedback. As a leader, it's a good idea to encourage people to feel more comfortable giving and receiving feedback. As you get to know your team members better, you will recognize how the individuals on your team react to feedback.

Having both positive, and the more difficult conversations, is a key skill of leadership. If feedback is used effectively in your team, you can increase motivation and improve performance. It will encourage continuous learning and increase confidence for the team members.

When feedback is given constructively, people will often respond positively. It follows that if it's done infrequently or poorly, the opposite results will occur.

Some people can get defensive when they receive feedback, and some may even feel a sense of failure. For others, actively seeking feedback and constantly wanting to improve is less intimidating, and they may be less sensitive to receiving constructive feedback. We all have different baselines and recovery times when we receive feedback.

You not only need to learn to give feedback effectively, with care and skill, but you also need to help the team members you lead to consider feedback as the norm in their team culture. Coaching them to recognize the value of feedback for self-improvement, and the impact on their work, will be important.

Allow Room for Reflection

Give people time to reflect on what you are saying when you give feedback. Sometimes people need to take in the information and think it through for themselves. Allow people the time to process what you're telling them and to think about how they can make changes.

It is best to provide feedback as soon as possible, and as close to the situation or activity you want to talk about. It also needs to be specific and not general.

For example, 'Good job!' following a presentation would be more helpful if you were specific, for example:

TIPS ON FEEDBACK

Ask for permission to give feedback.
Provide context.
Be specific.
Don't expect everyone to respond.
Give it regularly.
Be honest and empathetic.
Ensure it's a two-way conversation.
Listen.
Make it private.
Be generous with appreciation.
Let people know you know what they do.
Be constructive not negative.
Acknowledge improvements.
Clarify expectations.
Don't make it personal.
Follow up.
Help to improve and build on.
Develop actions and goals.

'The introduction you gave was excellent, and you answered the clients' questions really thoroughly today, it has made a positive impact on the relationship.'

Ask Questions

Ask questions to make sure recipients feel listened to and give them the opportunity to suggest things themselves. Also, be prepared to offer suggestions. One of the keys to giving effective feedback is that it's got to be meaningful.

Ask for Permission

It's also a good idea to ask permission when giving feedback, firstly it gives people an opportunity to feel better prepared to be open to it, and secondly it helps your relationship, because this is a conversation intended to support. For example:

'I'd like to chat about yesterday's presentation, is it OK for us to discuss how it went now?'

'I've had a call from one of the directors about his laptop crashing and how he felt it went, can we chat about this at lunch time please?'

Team members have told us that it makes them anxious when a leader bumps into them in the corridor and says,

'I need to give you some feedback!'

So be specific: It's also a wise idea to remember to publicly praise but privately discuss feedback.

PROVIDING FEEDBACK UPWARD

Andrew, a management consultant, was asked to interview ten senior members at a company to see how they felt about their team culture and the individuals in it.

During the feedback session, Andrew started to read through a list of some of the points the team had raised. Beatrice, the chief executive who engaged Andrew, started to get agitated and finally called a halt to the meeting. She raised her concern that it was too negative and not indicative of the team's dynamic at all.

An awkward silence took over the room, and no one spoke for thirty seconds. Carl, a team member, piped in, challenging Beatrice's perception, 'But the people in this room are the only people who created this list and that's how we truly feel.'

At this point Beatrice asked Andrew to step outside. After a few minutes of internal discussion, Andrew was called back into the meeting, and eventually the team had an opportunity to look at their issues openly and focus on how to fix some things. Beatrice became part of the group, and additional honest communication from the team helped them move forward.

Providing feedback upward is important. Acting on this feedback in response to the team's input can be a gratifying experience for the entire group: it shows that the team's opinions are valued and respected.
—SM

Better in Person

If possible, always try to provide feedback in person. You can then text or email it to reinforce it, if appropriate. Always forward emails that you receive praising your team or individuals as soon as you can. Some people do appreciate having positive feedback written down. If, on the other hand, it is a team-wide issue, you can bring it up in a team meeting and invite everyone to offer suggestions for improvements.

It's important to help your team acknowledge the things they are good at, the things they are not so good at, seek meaningful feedback, and act on it. However, be sure not to overload people. Focus on a single issue, give the feedback, co-develop actions to effect changes, and then move on to any other issues or areas at the right time. If you don't, the individuals may feel under attack, which can be very demotivating.

Give feedback frequently, so it becomes part of the way the team does things but note that it's more difficult for recipients to acknowledge the feedback if they do not trust or respect you. As we've mentioned throughout the book, it is essential to build trust. As a leader, seek feedback about yourself too. There are some cultural differences in different organizations about giving feedback upward, but leaders miss something if they do not listen to their teams, and others, about things that they too could improve on.

Focus

Reinforce

Appreciate and Recognize

There are many organizations where positive feedback is not given frequently enough. The antidote is to take every opportunity to catch team members doing something right!

Appreciating what the team is accomplishing, the support they have given to one another, or an individual's efforts can all help to boost morale and productivity.

Both of us have worked in organizations where we have implemented activities to encourage appreciation of the whole team. Activities such as doughnut breaks—the leader buys them!—and coffee stops, where all the team members that are available have their breaks together. Don't forget the members who are otherwise occupied too. We also participated in 'brown bag lunches', where everyone brings their own lunch while someone presents a different topic or people chat informally. Activities such as birthdays and anniversaries can be celebrated.

We also introduced thank you boxes, with blank cards where the recipient's name can be inserted; anyone can thank anyone, either by leaving it

STORY A
ON THANKING THE FAMILY

Elisabeth traveled a great deal in one role she had in a global organization, and although her son **Fadel** was older, she had missed some key activities with him.

George, Elisabeth's boss at the time, sent Fadel gift vouchers for computer equipment, as he knew that he enjoyed computers and technology.

George wrote a letter saying how sorry he was to take Mom away, and she was doing a great job, and he appreciated Fadel's patience and support for Elisabeth. That was some decades ago, and Fadel still fondly remembers George's gesture, as does Elisabeth.

STORY B
A SINCERE THANK YOU?

Henrietta, the team leader, secluded herself behind her desk and sent emails to her team. The problem? All her team members sit directly outside her office! Henrietta avoids venturing into the open space if she can, but every Friday, when the team goes out to lunch together, she would quietly post encouraging notes on their monitors with expressions like, 'Atta boy!'

Instead of having the intended positive impact, the team found it annoying, and it quickly became an office joke.
—SM

on their desk or personally handing it to them. We mentioned these in chapter 7, too, where we suggested that these could be used to recognize people who live the organization's core values. We've seen people's faces light up when they get one unexpectedly.

Work out what each team member is interested in and reward them in a way that tells them you are interested in their interests.

A thank you is wonderful to receive and is not difficult to give. We should ask ourselves how frequently acknowledgments are made, and if they don't happen often enough, we need to address it. Be generous with positive and genuine recognition.

Be the leader who is known for acknowledging the contributions of others. Express your appreciation and show people that they are valued.

Take your ego out of the equation and give credit to the team. When talking to others about your teams' achievements, make it obvious that you are proud of them. Your reward will be a team that is healthy and happy. Work may not always be fun, but you can have fun doing it.

AVOIDING CONFLICT

Manage Conflict

One thing you won't escape from in the workplace is conflict. It's inevitable with the diversity of people involved in businesses. We cannot eradicate conflict, and we should not try. Healthy conflict expressing differing opinions and views can help to identify gaps, highlight issues, and provide alternatives that might not have been previously considered.

The key is to manage it carefully.

The stresses of modern business, with different personalities, different working styles, different customer service expectations, competing for resources and time, can often lead to tensions

Jack constantly avoided conflict and in conversations with his own leader, attempted to suggest that he was dealing with things.

By not encouraging the resolution of the conflicts and not having those difficult conversations, some of his team started to avoid working with each other and used other team members as conduits.

Jack was uncomfortable with any type of conflict, so instead of addressing the real issues, he tried moving people around.

This, however, impacted customer satisfaction and had an impact on other parts of the team who had been working well.

By not acknowledging the conflicts directly, Jack also made some assumptions about what had created the conflict. Eventually, when he discussed it with the relevant parties, he discovered other reasons that could have easily been dealt with.

The team was reshuffled again, but the lack of early intervention led to some key team members leaving the team, impacting the IT department.

There could have been a different outcome if the issues had been faced at the right time. It may feel difficult, but the team is more likely to respect you for dealing with issues as opposed to you denying anything is wrong, not making the right decisions and avoiding awkward conversations. —SM and conflict. Differing priorities in managing projects can also create tensions.But poor leadership can also lead to tensions, resulting in conflict between team members and their counterparts.

As a leader, managing conflict is a key competency to develop. Recognize tensions early on, and resolve them in a calm, controlled, and positive way. Sometimes conflict may arise when your team can't resolve a problem. Some tips might be to use brainstorming, encourage them to collaborate, meet all together, and revisit the goals that they had set. It's key to use your emotional intelligence to show empathy and listen. It's important for people to be heard when they feel conflicted.

Empower the Team

Coaching the team to resolve their own tensions and conflicts will also help build a healthier team.

It can help if you have an open-door policy, where team members feel free to chat with you, and others, in a safe and open environment, to help resolve issues. Encourage your team to apologize when conflicts arise due to someone making a mistake and be accountable. It also helps if the organization has policies in place to deal with issues like bullying or harassment. There may however be a time when you find it difficult to resolve some issues, and this is a good time for a third party or mediator to intervene.

Clarify Expectations

Ensure you have clear expectations communicated. For example, in the case of some end-user issues, a lack of service-level agreements will lead to a lack of accountability and tensions between parties with differing expectations. Over promising and not delivering is certain to create conflict too.

Put processes and policies in place and create standards. This will take away some of the inconsistencies which can create conflict. Provide clarity.

In your one-on-ones, you will gather information about potential conflict between team members and become aware of how people interact with each other. Use this intelligence to help coach team members to think about different ways they can address their issues.

Also, be aware of the person who enjoys playing the devil's advocate or using their own own voice to see how others react, as this is disrespectful and a waste of others' time. People relaying rumors should also be encouraged to find out the facts and not get involved.

Set expectations for how people should behave and be prepared to call them out when unmet. As we mentioned earlier, a set of guiding principles or core values can assist you in doing this more effectively.

You may have to get out of your comfort zone trying to resolve or manage

conflict but remember that avoiding or accommodating conflict will not make it disappear. Managing it more effectively will help you to create a healthier environment for your team to work in.

Delegate

Delegating is not about the redistribution of tasks. It is about assigning tasks and activities that will help individuals develop. Sometimes the workload might demand that some work is reassigned and the team work together to accomplish this, but delegation should be a process not a convenience.

If the organization needs teamwork to achieve its goals, you will need to invest time in developing the skills required and challenging the team. Know Your People (KYP). To delegate effectively, you must know your people well, their strengths and weaknesses, skills, and experience. This helps you to gauge how you approach delegation to help team members develop. Assign them tasks that will facilitate their development and ensure that these tasks are aligned with the overall goals.

Focus on the Team

Establishing clear expectations, support, and regular checkpoints are essential to this process. Some team members will require more assistance than others. Your leadership style will also change with each team member, depending on their competencies, their commitment, and the tasks involved. Some will: need directing, be enthusiastic, be less enthusiastic, need coaching and supporting, and others may be self-reliant.

ACRONYM
ALERT!

KYP

KNOW
YOUR PEOPLE

Essentially, you as the leader need to focus on your team members rather than workplace circumstances and adapt your leadership style according to the maturity of the team member.

One size does not fit all as we noted in the story of the 20-year leader earlier.

Challenge the team, but don't leave them without a support structure. If you build trust with the team, and they know you have their interests at heart, you can encourage them to challenge themselves more.

THE IMPACT OF YOUR
KEY TEAM

Amber, a newly hired CIO had several leaders reporting to her. When she inherited this team, she quickly discovered how fragmented the leadership was.

One leader, Batoul, communicated with her and shared concerns about other teams without involving other leaders.

Carlos, another leader, focused only on his team and avoided sharing negative information with his superiors. He was always defending his team, spending less time with the leadership team and more time with those reporting to him.

Another two members, Dalilah and Evelyn, relied on one another to solve problems, taking decisions without consulting the rest of the leadership team.

Feedback about any of the teams was typically perceived as criticism by the other leaders.

The groups below this level were clearly aware of the fractures in the leadership above as their lack of cohesion was evident and affected the day-to-day activities. Poor communication and siloed decision-making, for example, caused additional tension and a lack of accountability.

Despite successfully leading their own teams individually, as a team the leadership did not model good teaming practices.

To address the divisions and fragmentation, Amber introduced the idea of the **key team** and worked hard to pull the team together.

It took some time, but finally the leadership team was working together with a focus on their peers, resulting in better decision-making and communication. Once the team's thinking shifted, the business benefited, and the leadership team was able to take on larger responsibilities. It also allowed them to serve as role models for their teams. They also introduced this idea to their own teams.

Having a key team working together radically improved the cohesion, enabled the leadership to engage in more problem-solving, improve cross-team and collaboration. Amber was now able to focus on her strategic tasks as the CIO.

—YA+SM

Aim to Delegate

Ensure the individuals know to what extent they can make decisions and delegate the appropriate amount of authority, depending on the task and the individual. You may think you could do it better, or that you would have done it differently, but the team members need to feel trusted and learn from their own experiences. Ensure you build in regular updates, monitoring, and reviews, and that you debrief so that people can learn from increased responsibilities and opportunities.

In earlier chapters, we encouraged you to let go of doing things yourself, and this is particularly key to effective delegation. It is demotivating for the team if you try to get involved in everything. This behavior, no matter how well-intentioned, will not help them develop or allow you, the leader, to accomplish everything. Team members have told us that when they have been delegated tasks and then their leaders keep verifying their work, they lose trust in the leader, and they don't feel trusted either. You cannot delegate and micromanage; micromanaging undermines team members. Remember, as a leader you will always be accountable.

A Final Thought

A leader we both worked with presented us with a great insight into what he had learned about the key teams. It's a concept that we have found very effective in practice.

As a new leader, you may feel that all your attention must go to the team you are leading. **However, your own team of peers, the team you belong to and report to, is your key team.** If this team works well, it demonstrates cohesion, and serves as a model for the teams you lead. Your teams will notice any fractures with their leadership teams and these gaps can often prevent the teams that you lead from performing at their best.

Building strong peer relationships is critical because the IT department relies heavily on collaborative efforts within and across divisions to deliver value to businesses. These leader relationships help to improve decision-making and promote alignment at different levels of an organization.

Developing others is a rewarding leadership activity.

Carefully assess the skills and knowledge of the team and use all the resources available to you to support them.

Work with people on their personal development plans in partnership.

Delegate for development.

Create an environment where feedback is solicited and acted upon, for all the team, including you as leader.

Stay close to issues but distant enough to manage performance.

You need to address and manage conflict to positively impact mo-rale, produc-tivity, and your own growth as a leader.

A leader is also part of their own leadership team with their own development needs.

AND NOW FOR SOMETHING DIFFERENT

Information
technology
and business
are becoming
inextricably
interwoven.
I don't think
anybody can talk
meaningfully
about one
without talking
about the other.

BILL GATES

IT Is Not About Technology

In the previous chapters, we focused on the human element of leadership. Now we are going to present something to complete the story.

To lead a technical team effectively, you must also focus on several other aspects to strengthen your leadership.

Although technology, for technology's sake, can be rewarding, organizations develop and implement technical solutions to solve real-world problems to accomplish specific goals.

As obvious as this might seem, many engineers and technical leaders sometimes forget that.

Most techies tend to spend their time seeking the most elegant and perfect solution to a technical challenge while all the end-user needs are 'optimal' solutions to their real-world problems.

The end-user does not care if you can implement their solution with the fewest lines of code or the coolest objects or even if you use containers or not. They certainly don't care if you run on Linux, Ubuntu, Windows or your own operating system.

What they care about is that the payroll gets done on time, all the time, without errors, and that the business has a technical solution to sell to their clients. They care, for example, that students can register for courses with no complaints and that patients are well cared for.

Engage with the Business

The challenge with leading a strong technical team is that many of the team members are more interested in the technical elegance of their solution than they are in addressing the 'business' problem at hand. We started the book by suggesting IT professionals today need good business acumen and that they often present two sides of the beast. In this chapter, we look at ways you, as a new leader, can engage with the business and deliver more successfully.

Because the techie will focus on the solution to their issues, many will spend days and nights trying to select and develop the perfect solution. However, there is never a perfect solution. Furthermore, a platform that is ideal from a technical point of view may not be what the market needs.

Your job as a technical team leader is to find the right balance between technical elegance and relevance to your stakeholders.

Develop Requirements, Don't Gather Them

Part of your job as a technical team leader is to understand your stakeholder's fundamental needs and keep them focused on what is important.

It is normal to want to serve your stakeholders and meet their every wish. However, you don't have infinite resources to meet their ever-changing wants.

Yes, their wants, not needs. When you go to gather requirements, you ask your stakeholder, 'What do you need? What do you want?'

This, in our opinion, is a losing strategy. The fact is (and don't say this too loud) most stakeholders have no clue what they need from the technology solutions you can provide.

However, your stakeholders know very well what they need accomplished and what prevents them from doing so. For example, they might see that they have a problem with signing up customers, and they may translate that to I 'need a red button on the right to make it faster', when in fact, a simple workflow change could fix the problem much more effectively.

I WANT MY OWN LAB!

A social scientist once approached us, wanting to build a lab with 50 computers. Instead of gathering the requirements for this lab by asking, 'what kind of computers? What kind of software do you need? Who will be using them?' We took the approach of asking him, "What is it you are trying to do? And what are your pain points?" By asking that question, we learned that he was conducting a survey of thousands of people and wanted to hire students to collect the information, capture it in excel, and then purchase software to analyze the data. After discussing the scientist's needs with the team, we realized that building a lab with 50 computers was not the best approach to solving this problem. Instead of spending his grant on building a lab and equipping it with computers, we proposed that he use a portion of that grant to expand our high-performance cluster with a few more nodes and use the rest of his grant to increase the pay of his research assistants. By doing so, he collected and processed his data more efficiently by hiring a more motivated team of research assistants instead of data entry clerks. For our part, we expanded our HPC cluster, which other researchers could use. This also helped reduce our design, implementation, and support resources.
—YA

So, instead of asking your stakeholders

 What do you need? What do you want?

you really need to ask them,

 What do you do? What are your pain points?

Put yourself in their shoes, try to understand their day-to-day pain points, and dig deep into the root cause of the issue to develop the requirements and the appropriate solutions.

Unless you focus on understanding the fundamental challenges that the stakeholder is trying to address, it is very easy for you to waste your team's resources on developing less relevant solutions.

All Solutions Are Permanent

Systems have ways of growing tentacles. No matter where you start or how clear you are about how temporary your solution is, over time, the systems you deploy will expand in scope, grow with users, and become harder and harder to retire.

Prioritize buying over development

So, make your system choices wisely by considering the full life cycle. Pay special attention to post-deployment support. That means you should probably buy and integrate off-the-shelf systems instead of developing your own. Off-the-shelf systems come with a large team behind them who will keep the features up-to-date and provide maintenance and support.

Another advantage of off-the-shelf systems, especially Software-as-a-Service (SaaS) applications, is the limited ability to customize. Although this might seem like a disadvantage at first glance, forcing your users to use standardized processes and workflows is a good thing.

In addition to reducing operational and support costs, it allows you to focus your resources on integration, data extraction, and analysis instead of keeping up with the ever-changing end-user needs. This approach also encourages your stakeholders to use best practices in their business.

Select Platform Based on Local Support

When you choose your platforms, make sure to keep operational support needs in mind. In our view, most platforms are technically similar.

Over time, the functional, performance, and security gaps between them become smaller and smaller. Therefore, a key factor in choosing the appropriate platform lies in the availability and cost of local quality post-production support.

Provide Recommendations Not Options

As a technical team leader, you are seen by your peers and stakeholders as the technology expert.

Although your stakeholders may claim that their 9-year-old nephew can do your job better than you ever could—yes, we've had this said to us!— they really want you to relieve them from all the pesky details of getting their technology needs addressed.

WHO THE HECK DID YOU SEND ME?

Kat, the CEO wanted to revamp the boardroom and asked Lou, the CIO to engage his team in the technical design.

Lou assigned Jack to lead a cross-functional IT team in developing and presenting a solution to the CEO.

Right after the presentation, Kat called Lou: 'Who the heck did you send me? What kind of team do you have? If your team can't design a simple system, I might as well fire you all!'

So, after looking into the matter, the CIO discovered that Jack had developed a detailed and well-thought-out design. He had led members of the AV, network, and systems teams to come up with robust and creative alternatives to meet the CEO's needs.

The issue was not with the solution or the team's technical expertise but it was with the way the solution was presented to the CEO.

In a typical engineering manner, Jack presented Kat with multiple options. For each option, Jack presented the pros and cons, cost aternatives, and potential risks.

Despite everything they say, they are really looking to you for solutions. The challenge, of course, is that there is no perfect solution.

Every proposal comes at a price and with some risks, whether functional, financial, political or otherwise. As solution providers, we need to develop options and understand the advantages, disadvantages, costs, and risks of each solution we come up with. By creating alternative options, we typically also develop a deeper understanding of the alternatives and a sense of the 'optimal' approach.

When Kat asked questions, Jack explained in detail the potential outcomes for each available option. But all the CEO wanted to know was, 'What is the solution? How much does it cost? And what are the risks?'

But instead, she got overwhelmed with options and details that she did not understand and felt that she was being 'bamboozled' by an incompetent team.

To fix things, Lou coached Jack: 'Next time you meet with the CEO, present your one recommended solution. Show her the functionality, costs, and critical issues of this solution. You don't have to go into the details or list the cons unless you are asked. Keep all the other options and details 'in your back pocket'. If Kat says your solution is too expensive, you can show an alternative to reduce the cost and what that will mean in terms of function and risk. If the CEO wants additional features, you can then present an alternative and what the implications are on cost and risk, and so on.'

After the next meeting with Jack, Kat called Lou again: 'I don't know what you did, but Jack and the team were amazing! They were confident and knew exactly what they were talking about! After a very efficient discussion, I got the solution I need at the right costs and risks.'

And no, the CIO did not get a bonus.
—YA

But just because we do our analysis and develop options, we don't have to confuse the stakeholder with all of them. In fact, we should not.

Remember, you are expected to be the expert, and the stakeholders look to you for advice. If you are a non-technical leader, seek guidance from your technical team or bring someone with you to meetings where technical advice will be provided.

Don't Over-Complicate It

Presenting all possible options to stakeholders at once and asking them to make a decision can diminish their perception of your competence and makes them feel that you don't know your domain and are avoiding accountability. It also asks them to take on the responsibility of making choices they don't quite understand.

As a leader, it is advisable to suggest an 'optimal' solution instead of presenting all options to the stakeholder.

When the stakeholder brings up costs or other concerns, you can offer your alternatives as possible solutions to those problems.

By taking this approach, you not only help the stakeholder focus on what is essential, but you also present yourself as the expert you are and build trust by taking accountability for some of those decisions.

No Such Thing as a Free Lunch

We were told by a colleague once that most folks who work in IT do so because they love technology and love to help people. It is precisely these two traits that get IT teams in trouble all the time. End users will always ask for something, change their minds, ask for something different, and then ask for more.

In the meantime, your team scrambles from one requirement to another, trying to keep up with the whims of the end users. The irony is that the more responsive your team is, the greater the number of requests from end users.

The end users continuously underestimate what it takes to meet their requests and are disappointed when IT can't meet their escalating wants.

As a team leader, you must satisfy end users' needs (not wants) while helping them understand the effort involved in managing your load and their expectations.

One approach is to break down your deliverables into small chunks that your team can deliver quickly. By doing so, your end-user gets something valuable they can benefit from quickly.

As importantly, by not investing too much time in the small chunks, you have little to 'throw away' when the end-user changes their mind, and you have more flexibility with handling new priorities as they come up.

Although this method allows for flexibility in adapting to changing requirements, it doesn't consider the costs of meeting them. In addition, the end-user may perceive the requests as simple, encouraging them to request additional changes that do not benefit the organization.

To better manage the flow of 'change requests', it is important for you to help the end users understand the costs—in time, scope, and budget—involved in making such changes.

DEC WHO?

The sad truth is that most people reading this book don't recognize or remember who DEC is.

DEC—or Digital Equipment Corporation—was, for the longest time, the second-largest computer company in the world.

DEC invented, or was a key contributor, to many of the technologies we use today. This includes virtual memory, multi-user operating systems, Ethernet, the Alpha chip, and many others.

DEC computers were probably the best computers ever designed from an engineering perspective. In fact, one could argue that many 'new technical features' that you see in devices today were implemented by DEC back in the 1970s, 1980s, and 1990s.

The focus was always on building the best-engineered products. That included everything from hardware to firmware, operating systems, applications, and mechanical systems. In fact, DEC computers even went through rigorous 'shake and bake' testing to ensure that they worked under the most extreme conditions.

But DEC's fatal flaw was that it was a company of engineers.

DEC focused intensely on the technical aspects of their designs at the expense of the 'market needs'.

Although engineers loved DEC's equipment, the company was not able to compete in the 'business and consumer' market and was finally broken up with different pieces being acquired by various other companies such as Intel and Compaq, which was bought by HP.
—YA

The best way to accomplish this is to involve end users in the decision-making process and have them 'pay' a portion of the costs associated with each change.

That means you should never accept a change request without extracting a cost out of the customer—even if it is symbolic.

For instance, if the end-user requests a last-minute change in functionality, you may inform them that this will incur a delay or require an additional budget.

Being responsive 'for free' devalues your team's efforts and encourages the end user to underestimate what it takes to deliver, resulting in more frivolous requests and greater disappointments. Therefore, it is important to be aware of your team's tasks and that you have frequent checkpoints to monitor their progress.

IT Is About Making Decisions

When left to their own devices, most technical staff would prefer to spend their time-solving technical problems.

This, in turn, could lead to endless design, development, and testing cycles as a technical staff is never satisfied until they have a perfect product—something that we all know is not achievable.

It is up to the leader of a technical team to make the call on when the design is good enough or when the code is stable enough, and when the service is ready for roll-out into production.

Of course, this takes deep knowledge of the business environment, detailed technical knowledge of the product being developed, trust in the team, and, most importantly, confidence and courage to make the 'we are done' call.

While delaying the release to minimize failure is a safer way to go, waiting too long before providing the service can harm your business and, as importantly, your faith in your team's

ability to deliver. We must acknowledge that there isn't a perfect solution. There is no bug-free technology. And in most circumstances, there aren't any 'life-and-death' technical decisions that are too costly to change if they are wrong.

We also must acknowledge that a 'no decision' is also a decision. By not deciding to release a product, you have decided to delay. By not deciding to stop testing, you have decided to extend the evaluation.

Being a leader means being accountable. And accountability requires making decisions. So, how do you decide when to decide?

For that, we would like to paraphrase General Colin Powell's 'Lesson 15' from his *A Leadership Primer* presentation. We call it the 70/40 rule. Notice that the numbers don't add up to 100! Powell suggests that if you have enough data to ensure a 40% chance of success, then you should proceed. If you wait until you have enough data to secure a 70% chance of success, you have waited too long. The point of this rule is making a quick, decisive decision is always better than waiting too long.

The 70/40 are not cast in stone—you can pick any two numbers that make sense in your environment. What matters is that you have a cutoff that allows you to make decisive and relatively quick decisions.

Process Does Not Mean Bureaucracy

Part of your job as a technical team leader is to figure out when to stop development and go into testing. And when to stop testing and go into production, how to respond to requests and emergencies, and how to ensure your systems are safe and available.

For that, you need a small set of simple processes—a set of tools and guidelines that help you become faster and better at what you do. If you find a process slowing you down, you should refine it rather than discard or ignore it.

There are many models to help you with that— some more agile than others— based on different philosophies. On the one hand, you have the conservative approach of 'do it right the first time,' and on the other, you have the agile philosophy of 'fail fast, fail often'. Each of those has a time and place.

MEATLOAF LORE

JOHNNY
Mommy, why do you cut off the end of the meatloaf when you bake it in the oven?

MOTHER
I don't know, Johnny dear, my Mother taught me. Go ask her.

JOHNNY
Grandma, why do you cut off the end of the meatloaf when you bake it in the oven?

GRANDMOTHER
I don't know, Johnny dear, my Mother taught me. Go ask her.

JOHNNY
Great-Grandma, why do you cut off the end of the meatloaf when you bake it in the oven?

GREAT-GRANDMOTHER
Oh, Johnny dear, it's because when we first got married, we had a tiny oven.

Just because it's been done this way for ever, it doesn't mean it's the best way to do it. Question processes before implementing them in systems.
—YA

Depending on your organization and the maturity of your team, you may wish to consider one, both, or a combination of the two.

It is tempting for new leaders to implement 'best practice' frameworks such as CMMI, COBIT, ITIL, and others fully. But that would be a mistake.

In addition to the required time and effort to establish such frameworks, simply implementing them without truly understanding their fundamental principles and adapting them to your organization would be like 'cutting your meatloaf before baking it'.

Unless your industry requires it, we believe obtaining high levels of certification in these frameworks is not always necessary.

All frameworks have fundamental components that you can adapt and apply in your organization.

The trick is to grasp the core concepts of a proposed project and then establish the bare minimum structure required to align with your organization's culture and objectives.

It is also worth noting that you can't solve problems with technology alone. This is particularly true when it comes to securing your data and systems. *People are the weakest link in all attacks.* Using technology is only part of the defense. Instituting and enforcing the appropriate policies and procedures are fundamental to protecting yourself.

Joe joined a software company that had not issued a new release for two years. He was tasked with getting the software development back on track. Joe noticed that the team was busy developing new features while the current release had more than 3,000 bugs. For some reason, folks thought adding more features to an unstable product would make it sell more. So, Joe took the bold decision and stopped the development of all new features until all critical bugs had been addressed. But resolving 3,000 bugs is not a joke. Besides, there is no such thing as bug-free code. So, when can Joe deem the code 'stable'?

After discussions, Joe and the team defined a subset of the bugs as 'critical' and used the 'zero critical bugs' as the criterion for 'good enough to ship' and set off to tackle these bugs one at a time. But just defining 'what is good enough' is not sufficient. Joe had to put processes in place to ensure that all these bugs were properly addressed before release and before anyone could start working on new features. The process was quite simple. Each morning, Jane, the QA engineer, listed all critical bugs on a whiteboard in the company kitchen. Then, Joe met with the team and assigned a set of critical bugs to each engineer. Joe also instituted the rule, 'It isn't fixed until Jane takes it off the board.' The competition between the engineers and their desire to move on to developing new features got the team through the critical bugs in no time. The bottom line is this:

If you set criteria to help your team focus on what is critical and then institute processes to ensure they follow through, magic happens.

Oh, I almost forgot: Joe was able to reduce the product release cycle from two years down to three weeks—all within three months of implementing his changes.
—YA

WHEN IS GOOD ENOUGH GOOD ENOUGH?

IT is About Problem Solving

IT is about solving real-world problems using technology. You are the expert, and as such, you are expected to provide the stakeholder with recommendations and not ask them for one. Remember that any system you install will be there indefinitely. When choosing your systems, focus on integration and support.

Put processes in place to ensure consistency. But make sure your processes match your environment.

Talking to the team about these issues and explaining your decision-making process can be beneficial. There is a wealth of useful topics that you can introduce into your team meetings, regardless of whether you are a technical or a non-technical leader. This will prove to be very helpful to you in your new leadership role.

Now that you have these ideas take some time to apply them in a mindful way. Consider some of the areas we have discussed: your environments, the businesses you serve, your development as a leader and the development of your team, and the other people and parts of the organization with whom you must connect, relate, and engage.

Enjoy a journey that will be both fulfilling and challenging.

IT is not about technology.

IT is about solving real-world problems.

Dig deep to understand your users' needs, not wants.

You are the expert, so provide them with a recommendation and don't confuse them with options—keep those in your back pocket in case issues come up.

Don't give anything for free, and use the 2-out-of-3 rule to make them understand the effort it takes to deliver.

Things will change, so follow the 40/70 rule, and make quick decisions.

Don't spend your time trying to be perfect.

But also, avoid the Band-Aid fix—there are no temporary solutions.

Make sure to do all this with efficient and repeatable processes.

CASE STUDY
CLIMBING A MOUNTAIN

CASE STUDY 01

G2L
'Begin with the end in mind.'
STEPHEN COVEY
MISSION
VISION
Fisou Y. Tirtchun
Chief Information Office
0704 G2L 63/19

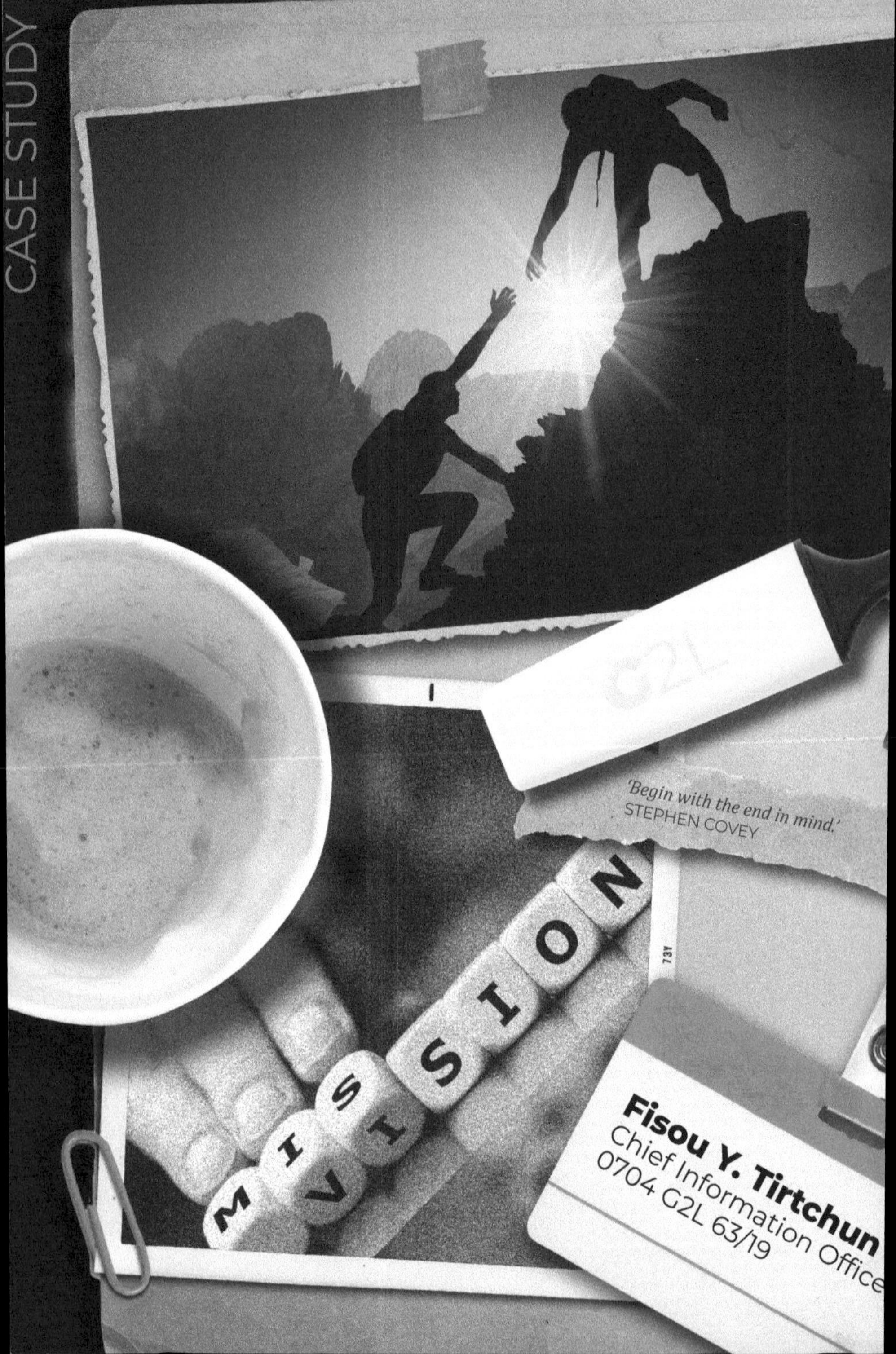

CLIMBING A MOUNTAIN FROM ROCK BOTTOM TO TRANSFORMATION PARTNER

Fisou, a new IT executive joined a large organization at a time when **everything was going wrong with IT.**

There were serious data breaches that leaked to the news and social media. The network was slow and unreliable. Server and storage infrastructure was at capacity and somewhat obsolete, and critical systems crashed regularly. They were at rock bottom.

But that was only half the story.

IT as an organization had just gone through a few years of leadership and structural changes that left the team devastated. The staff was completely demotivated, and in-fighting was rampant. There was a high level of anxiety across the IT team, and almost everyone was playing the "survival game" of hoarding information and avoiding blame.

Hardly anyone in the larger organization had anything good to say about IT.

Fisou, tasked with fixing IT, asked himself: "Where do I start?" And it dawned on him: "Of course, start at the beginning. **Let's go back to the basics.**" With that in mind, he set off on his journey.

Fisou had previously worked with organizations where leadership revolved around establishing a clear mission and making people the key focus (see Chapter 7).

As the leader in charge, he believed that his role was to clarify the mission, get the staff to work as a team, **align them around that mission**, and ensure that they were equipped with the tools to do their jobs while removing obstacles from their path. **So, instead of focusing on fixing the infrastructure, technology, and services, Fisou decided to start with the mission and people.**

By following many of the techniques and guidelines in this book, Fisou managed to **"fix IT" and turn it into a true transformation partner in record time.**

Case Study
Part 2.

ESTABLISH THE BASELINE

Fisou's first step was to **reduce anxiety within the team** and among all stakeholders by letting everyone know that he would establish a baseline before developing an organizational system or making service changes.

Given that IT had gone through a turbulent time, it made sense **not to make any changes before understanding the real issues,** their context, and, most importantly, what the constraints were to make these changes.

However, he also knew that the organization could not wait much longer, and significant service improvement had to be done quickly.

So, he applied General Powell's "40/70" rule, ensuring he spent just enough time and effort to assess the situation before making changes and quickly formulated the three-year road-map in his head.

With this road-map in mind, he spent nearly all of the first few weeks meeting with each of his 100+ staff and 20+ business unit leaders. He used these meetings to accomplish **three objectives.**

1. The first objective was **to listen attentively to everyone** to learn more about the organization, understand everyone's concerns, and, most importantly, gain insight into the team and stake-holder relation-ships and "politics".

2. His second objective was to use these meetings **to set expectations.** He used the initial meetings with staff to establish his expectations for teamwork, information sharing, timeliness, and quality of work. During his meetings with the other stakeholders, he made it clear that change would take time and

'Courage is what it takes to stand up and speak; Courage is also what it takes to sit down and listen!'
WINSTON CHURCHILL

sought their patience, help, and support. In addition, **by listening-to-understand, and seeking their support,** he used these stakeholder meetings to assert a foundation on which to **build trust and give stakeholders some ownership in the success of IT.**

3. The third objective was to **identify the key priorities and key players.** Fisou needed to quickly determine the team members who could be relied upon to get things moving and those who may undermine any change. He also needed to quickly **identify the most significant stakeholders, their pain points, and who could lend him and his team the needed support.** This would help him understand the potential allies, organizational priorities, and

challenging areas, which would help them clarify the team's objectives.

A positive consequence of the staff meetings was that **several staff members suggested a few ideas** that Fisou had not considered. **He enthusiastically added them to the plan and credited the team members** who came out with them. By doing so, Fisou was not only able to get new ideas on the table but also to get buy-in and excitement across the team. **The staff felt that they were being heard and took ownership of the ideas.**

The 40/70 Rule

Part I: "Use the formula P=40 to 70, in which P stands for the probability of success and the numbers indicate the percentage of information acquired".

Part II: "Once the information is in the 40 to 70 range, go with your gut."

Don't take action if you have only enough information to give you less than a 40 percent chance of being right, but don't wait until you have enough facts to be 100 percent sure, because by then it is almost always too late. Today, excessive delays in the name of information-gathering breeds "analysis paralysis". Procrastination in the name of reducing risk actually increases risk!

Case Study
Part 3.

CREATE A STRONG TEAM IDENTITY

mission statement and a set of core values. He then handed the drafts to a small group of his staff to refine. By doing so, **he encouraged teamwork among his key players and, at the same time, got their buy-in.** The group worked-- sometimes on their own, and other times with Fisou--for a few weeks. Upon completion, and to **increase engagement,** each group member was tasked with leading a larger group of staff in finalizing the mission statement and core values.

'Teamwork is the ability to work together toward a common vision. The ability to direct individual accomplishments toward organizational objectives.'

ANDREW CARNEGIE

The endless meetings and tons of coffee paid off. Within a relatively short time and by working with and getting the buy-in of key staff he could depend on, Fisou was able to **develop and begin executing a transformation plan.**

The first thing he did was **establish a strong identity for the team.** He did that by drafting a

Based on an idea a team member proposed, Fisou asked a visually skilled member to **translate the mission and core values into compelling posters and memorable objects.** Fisou then gathered everyone in **regular town hall meetings to share and reinforce** the mission, **core values, priorities, and procedures.** He also made sure to frequently update the entire team on progress results and concerns.

PRIORITY MATRIX

In parallel, Fisou **built a priority matrix** outlining the importance and urgency of key issues and services that must be addressed. He divided the priorities into three areas: **People, Process,** and **Systems,** and categorized them based on their **level of urgency.** Fisou shared the matrix with his stakeholders and his team. He ensured **everyone was focused on the critical issues** and regularly updated the matrix.

During his specific business-focused one-on-ones, Fisou also learned that most trust and morale issues were related to **saying "yes" too often.** By trying to please everyone all the time, the IT team

inadvertently over-promised and under-delivered, while being overwhelmed with unattainable targets. This led him to establish a few core processes and multi-functional "boards" that consisted of different team members. **The boards acted as "gates" to help prioritize requests and manage the workload.**

Going forward, all requests for new functionality or services had to go through the Request Review Board. The RRB's main function was to ensure choosing the right technology platform to **avoid "one-off" development and customization, and to ensure integration.** The RRB also played the role of confirming that delivery schedules were based on resource load and availability.

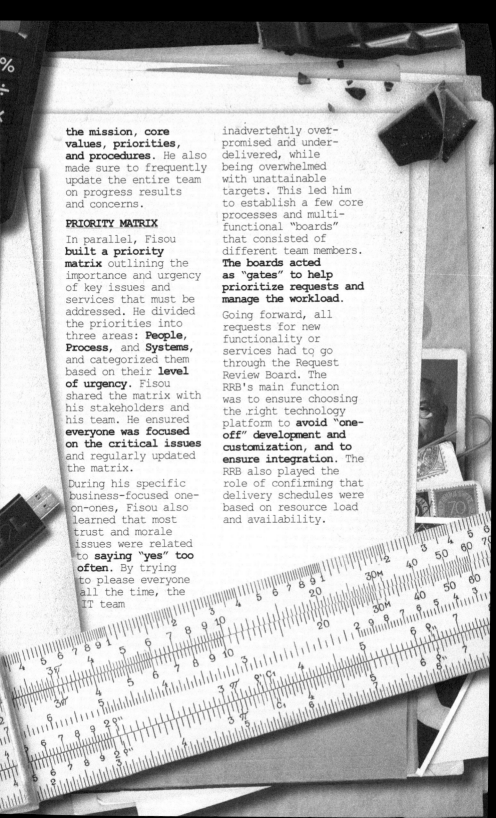

[1] Although Fisou did not dictate deadlines, **he insisted that staff take their schedule commitments seriously.** By making the reports public, he ensured that his **team was accountable for their commitments.**

[2] Fisou developed a reputation that **he responded to all his emails within 24 hours.**

[3] While Fisou allowed **a respectful and jovial atmosphere** in the workplace--his staff joked that all he did was "walk around and drink coffee"--he also let the team know that **he "meant business".**

'One thing more important than hiring good people quickly is getting rid of bad-fit quicker.'
BOARD MEMBER

KEEPING
TRACK
OF
EVERYTHING

Fisou soon established **"ticket tracking"** to manage all IT requests, whether they were support, enhancements, or new services. He implemented the **"If-it-is-not-in-the-system-it-doesn't-exist"** rule to ensure visibility on everything performed and to allow his management team to regulate the workload.

Fisou also **generated weekly reports** to track progress of all issues, enhancements, and projects[1]. After all, **"You get what you measure"**. Although the team initially expressed a level of discomfort, they eventually understood the value of accountability. The increased visibility and frequency of updates helped **build trust and responsibility**.

To ensure the high quality of service to the organization, Fisou reinforced the importance for all implemented requests and services to go **through the Control Review Board before they could be rolled out to the stakeholders**. The CRB, like the RRB (see previous section), is a cross-functional team and acts as the **quality control gate before any release**. By ensuring all services went through the CRB, Fisou ensured that **everyone took ownership of service quality**.

In addition to setting priorities and establishing procedures, Fisou raised his leadership level to **inspire everyone to focus on the mission**. He strove to safeguard the team by making sure they had the tools and information needed to excel at their task. Additionally, he continued working with the organizational stakeholders to **remove any remaining obstacles that could hinder the mission**.

In particular, the executive continued to **"be present"** [see Chapter 5]. He made sure to **drop by his team frequently and regularly, kept his door open, and quickly responded to questions and concerns**.[2]

Fisou continued to openly **keep track of team and individual progress**.[3] He would call staff into his office when he noticed behaviors inconsistent with the now-established core values. **He addressed such attitudes and slip-ups promptly**. Instead of reprimanding them, he worked closely with the people going off course to help them better understand their transgression and inspire new approaches to address it. However, for those few who were unable to or chose not to improve, **he took a firm and measured decision to let them go**.

Case Study
Part 5.

SEEK ADVICE AND PROMOTE LEADERS

While doing all this, Fisou also **cultivated the potential leaders on the team.** He engaged with Dyna, an external and highly-qualified coach and leadership consultant, to develop his reinvigorated team. **With Dyna's help, Fisou identified a handful of potential leaders on his team and put them through a nine-month** leadership training and coaching program.

Based on long discussions with Dyna, Fisou was able to eliminate the old and extended leadership team he inherited. **He reduced the direct team reporting to him to a smaller, more effective senior leadership team.** Part of the analysis helped identify some key members of the old leadership team as effective day-to-day managers and implementation champions. It was clear their contribution would be of more value in tactical leadership roles rather than in strategic positions.

It took some time, and gradually **people started feeling recognized for their value and efforts, and not just for their titles or pecking order. Dyna focused on re-instilling trust in the teams and facilitated individual growth and development.** At one point, the entire IT department went through a personal development program, and as a result and new insights, some of them chose to switch roles to better fit their interests and

VISITOR PASS

Dyna S. Follster
Consultant
2506 G2L 52/19

Valid until 19 FEBRUARY

'The function of leadership is to produce more leaders, not more followers.'
RALPH NADER

skills. This flexibility and awareness led to them scoring higher job satisfaction results while adding value to the company.

Both Fisou and Dyna soon noticed what the executive called the "hero syndrome". In one workshop session, Dyna gave this feedback to the new leadership group, who acknowledged that this was repetitive behavior. **While the teams mainly worked in silos, they often came together during a crisis.** The group was proud of how they collaborated to solve problems, which in most cases resulted from their vertical structure. Once the crisis was over, the teams went back to working separately. Consequently, Fisou made this a priority to fix.

The senior leadership received help to build their teams and encourage interdependencies. Several influential team members were coached as well. The complaining subsided as the **seniors developed their individual teams while focusing on the "key" team, and trust grew between them.** One of the leaders even added IT communications to her regular role, resulting in high motivation and repetition, which was critical to instilling the values, mission, and teamwork. Repetition and consistency were key.

Fisou also invested much time in regular meetings with the key stakeholders. **He conducted frequent and regular one-on-one sessions with each of them, listening to their concerns, updating them on** progress, sharing plans and challenges with moving forward, and, importantly, seeking their input and advice. It is interesting to note that these meetings were difficult initially, as the stakeholders had many legitimate complaints. **However, once the stakeholders realized that they were being listened to and updated with reliable information,** the meetings that used to be adversarial soon became social events.

IT Is Not About Technology

Although building the team and fixing systems is a multi-year process, the organization began to feel the impact of these changes within a short period of time. In fact, within three months of Fisou taking charge, the whining within the IT department and the organizational complaints about IT stopped.

Although the systems were still not fixed and the services were still unreliable, using the leadership skills and tools outlined in this case study **eased the anxiety among the team and steadily built trust within the organization.** This allowed Fisou and his team to focus on fixing the technical issues.

The number of complaints about systems and services went down even though the only thing that changed were the relationships.

The IT team's journey continues with a mountain of more challenges and exciting opportunities. They can continue to develop their leadership and work as one IT team moving in the same direction.

We have made every reasonable effort to acknowledge the copyright permissions for materials we have used in this book. If we have omitted anything we apologize and will correct in the reprints of credit. Our problem was that with so many years of experience and having worked with some of the people we reference, it's difficult not to absorb some things and feel they are a part of your own knowledge base. We have tried to attribute anything we have referenced.

All photographs are licensed from Shutterstock except:

Page 1, Walid's portrait by American University of Beirut and Sandy's portrait by Dimitri Nicomanis.

Page 129, Letter photo by Sandy Molloy.

All book covers, pages ii, 2, 12, 49, 83, 95, 110, 118, 120, 147, and 167 by Hani Asfour.

FOREWORD

Godfrey Reggio. https://www.brainyquote.com/quotes/godfrey_reggio_355797

Heraclitus. https://www.quotemaster.org/author/Heraclitus

Margaret Thatcher. https://www.azquotes.com/quote/1092979

Seuss, Dr (Theodor Seuss Geisel). *Oh, the Places You'll Go!* Random House, 1990.

INTRODUCTION

Generation Z. A white paper study: https://www.swisslife-global.com, includes research conducted separately by **McKinsey and Accenture** on Gen Z and provides an informative overview of this generation, their views on their lives and expectations of their work and careers.

Pew Research Center. July 28, 2020, Children's engagement with digital devices, screen time.

Discover Tec. https://www.discovertec.com

Franc Viscuso. https://www.linkedin.com/in/frank-viscuso-7a974736/

John Maxwell. https://www.maxwellleadership.com/john-maxwell/

Henry Ford. https://www.thehenryford.org

Theodore Roosevelt. https://www.brainyquote.com/quotes/theodore_roosevelt_140484

Kiyosaki, Robert T. *Rich Dad Poor Dad: What the Rich Teach Their Kids that the Poor and Middle Class Do Not!* Page 195, Plata Publishing, 1997.

Larry Page. Google CEO, July 2022, https://www.brainyquote.com/quotes/larry_page_622181

Simon Mainwaring. Founder, CEO, Author, *We First.* https://www.brainyquote.com/quotes/simon_mainwaring_494037

John F Kennedy. https://www.brainyquote.com/quotes/john_f_kennedy_121068

Seuss, Dr (Theodor Seuss Geisel). *If I Ran the Zoo.* Random House, 1950.

Daniel Goleman. Author, psychologist, and science journalist. He is internationally known for his work on emotional intelligence. https://www.brainyquote.com/quotes/daniel_goleman_585888

Bill Gates. 2017. 'Four ways famous introverts Bill Gates and Warren Buffett can help you be a better boss.' Video, CNBC.

https://www.cnbc.com/2017/07/10/4-ways-famous-introverts-bill-gates-and-warren-buffett-can-help-you-be-a-better-boss.html

Bill Gates. https://quotefancy.com/quote/99748/Bill-Gates-Be-nice-to-nerds-Chances-are-you-ll-end-up-working-for-one

Urban Dictionary. 2022. https://www.urbandictionary.com/define.php?term=Nerd

Carl Jung. 1875–1961. Jung was a Swiss psychiatrist who proposed a theory of psychological types. The theories were later taken up and extended by **Katherine Briggs** and her daughter **Isabel Myers**. The Myers Briggs assessments and tests are still used today to help individuals and teams to look at people's preferences on how they deal and relate to others, how they process information, make decisions, and organize their lives.

CHAPTER 3

Steve Jobs. A pioneer of the personal computer, his drive and passion for technology led him to become a visionary. He led the development and launch of the iPod and iPhone. https://www.codeitbro.com/?s=Technology+by+itself+-doesn%E2%80%99t+-

make+leaders.+Technology+only+amplifies+true+leadership.

Dr Seuss. https://www.goodreads.com/quotes/554940-i-love-my-job-i-love-the-pay-i-love

Warren Bennis was an American scientist, organizational consultant, leadership expert and pioneer of contemporary leadership studies. https://www.brainyquote.com/quotes/warren_bennis_389912

Tom Peters is an American writer on business management practices. The accolades paid to him by academics, organizations and practitioners of leadership and business consulting are too many to quote. Virtually all of Tom Peters written and speech materials are available free to download at https://tompeters.com.

CHAPTER 4

Rob Goffee and Gareth Jones. *Harvard Business Review*. Sept–Oct 2000. 'Leading and Managing People: Why Should Anyone Be Led by You? What it takes to be an Authentic Leader'.

Peter Senge. 'Fifth Discipline Book Summary'. *The Fifth Discipline: The Art and Practice of the Learning Organization*. Peter Senge was a visionary who saw how the world was changing and why learning was a key driver to performance, way ahead of its time.

The Journal of Business Strategy (1999) named Peter Senge as one of the 24 people who have had the greatest influence on business strategy over the last 100 years.

Lance H K Secretan is a British-Canadian author of business books, best known for his work in leadership theory and how to inspire teams. https://quotesgram.com/lance-secretan-quotes

Daniel Goleman. 2005. *Emotional Intelligence: Why it Can Matter More Than IQ for Character, Health, and Lifelong Achievement.*

Stephen Covey. *The 7 Habits of Highly Effective People*. This book continues to be a bestseller for the simple reason that it ignores trends and pop psychology and focuses on timeless principles of fairness, integrity, honesty, and human dignity. One of the most compelling books ever written, *The 7 Habits of Highly Effective People*, has empowered and inspired readers for over 25 years. It also played a part in the transformation of millions of lives across all age groups and professions. No matter how competent a person is, they will not have sustained lasting success unless they can effectively lead themselves, influence, engage and collaborate with others and continuously improve and renew their capabilities. These elements are at the heart of personal, team, and organizational effectiveness. According to the Society for Human Resource Management's 2016 'Employee Job Satisfaction and Employee Report', relationships with colleagues were the number one contributor to employee engagement, with 77% of respondents listing workplace connections as a priority.

Chuck Wolfe. President C J Wolfe Associates LLC. https://cjwolfe.com.

George Couros. Innovative Teaching, Learning and Leadership Consultant. *The Innovators Mindset' and 'Innovate inside the Box.'*

Seuss, Dr (Theodor Seuss Geisel). *The Cat in the Hat*. Random House, 1957

Chapter 6. This was the initial communication for people joining Anthony Willoughby on his expeditions.

Dear Punter,

I am delighted you have expressed interest in participating in our African Three Peaks expedition. However, before you decide to sign up it is very important you realise, we are not professional tour 23 guides, mountaineering experts, or doctors, we are punters like you. And if you do come along, you must be willing to get fit, pull your weight and fully understand you are there entirely at your own risk and choice.

This trip to the three African massifs with peaks more than 5,000 metres is going to be tough and challenging even for those who do not attempt the actual summits. The above said, those coming are not a group of Outward-Bound fanatics but a varied collection of expatriate British and a few presentable colonials and continentals who have decided to get together for a unique adventure, where the quality of the wine and company will usually be more important than getting to the top.

How difficult will it be? What will it be like? Frankly I do not know. I have never been on the mountains before, but all I have read and heard leads me to believe that it will be quite a trip. Overleaf you will find several regulations for coming on a Willoughby adventure.

I do not expect you to sign the document, but I do expect you to read it carefully and basically agree to the reasoning behind each of the 'regulations'. I hope you will consider coming along. Yours,

Anthony Willoughby

Patrick Lencioni. *Teamwork: The Five Dysfunctions of a Team*. The Table Group. https://www.tablegroup.com/

William Shakespeare. *Hamlet*. Act 1 Scene 3. https://literarydevices.net/to-thine-own-self-be-true/

CHAPTER 5

Stephen Covey. *The 7 Habits of Highly Effective People.*

Kahlil Gibran. *Sand and Foam. Alfred A. Knopf, 1926.*

Roy T Bennett. *The Light in the Heart.* 2016

Abraham Lincoln. https://www.azquotes.com/quote/176074

Aristotle. https://quotekind.com/authors/aristotle-excellence-quotes-to-achieve-goals/

Kipling, Rudyard. 'The Elephant Child'. *Just So Stories.* MacMillan, 1902

Sincere thanks to **Rabih Haidar** for allowing us to use his reflections on

how he developed emotional intelligence to build on his leadership skills.

Thanks also to **Alain Richard,** a Vice President who was a great leader to work with.

CHAPTER 6

Ken Robinson. *The Element.* Penguin, 2009

Colin Powell. 'General Colin Powell's Leadership Primer'. https://ung.edu/institute-lead-

ership-strategic-studies/_uploads/files/colin-powell-leadership.pdf. General Colin Powell whose decades long career made history, often quoted on his leadership philosophy.

Forrest Gump. Wikipedia. https://en.wikipedia.org/wiki/Forrest_Gump

Albert Einstein. https://www.goodreads.com/quotes/7256572-i-fear-the-day-that-technology-will-surpass-our-human

I WILL NOT COMPLAIN

IF I GET EATEN OR TRODDEN ON BY ANIMALS.
I understand that all attempts will be made to see that this does not happen.

IF EXTRA PORTERS ARE EMPLOYED WITH THE SOLE RESPONSIBILITY OF CARRYING WINE.
Because I know at the end of the day a bottle of wine always goes down well regardless of the situation.

IF OVERALL THE TRIP HAS A GENERAL AIR OF BRITISH AMATEURISM.
But I accept the importance and cost of using professionals whenever necessary, especially on the mountains.
I understand that most of these experiences will be very new to Willoughby as well.

IF THE TRIP DOES NOT GO TOTALLY TO PLAN.
I realize we are going to areas which even today are still very remote.

I also know that due to the very nature of Africa regulations can and often do change by the minute.

IF I DO NOT LIKE ANY DECISION OF THE LEADER.
Whether that leader is Willoughby or is appointed on the mountain; overall I expect decisions will be made jointly by everyone. But I accept that it is essential before any trip to understand that there is an undisputed leader.

IF I DO NOT GET EIGHT HOURS OF SLEEP IN A COMFORTABLE BED EVERY NIGHT.
I rather enjoy having no idea where I will spend the next night, be it in the back of a truck or under a palm tree.

IF I HAVE FORGOTTEN SOMETHING.
I will not endlessly ask people if they have got one, either I will bring it or shut up.

IF I DISCOVER I HAVE PRIMA DONNA TENDENCIES.
Regardless of my misconception of my importance and status in life, if I come on an I Will

Not Complain experience it is because I want to and do so of my own free will. At all times I will do my best to pull my weight.

IF THE WEATHER IS NOT WONDERFUL THE WHOLE TIME.
Or if I get cold, wet, and miserable. Because I will always have a spare set of warm clothes with me.

IF I COMPLAIN
I realise that I can be sent home. However, I understand that understated observations are permissible. For example, if I have frostbite, I am allowed to comment: 'Good heavens, it's a bit chilly, two of my toes have just turned black!'

It was not my intention to make the trip so tough that everyone would want to complain. I simply wanted to make those coming realise that travelling, like life, is not always as enjoyable as in our brochures. We wanted people who desired 'experience' which was special. I wanted to avoid complainers.
It had become blatantly obvious that complaining is the ultimate cardboard box. Those complaining usually are people who do not have the confidence to see a bold idea through. They simply tell everyone else about the danger and why it will not work. They are people whose nagging and lack of personal commitment can destroy the morale of any team, group, or organisation. Their negative behaviour can mean death on an expedition; they should be avoided at all costs. The people I sought were those who accepted the risks and understood the realities before they signed up. Once they signed up, they would accept the responsibilities which came with that commitment. They would be amongst a group of likeminded friends, and not pampered passengers. They would be people who realised and respected their total insignificance in the face of Mother Nature.

Timothy Leary. https://www.azquotes.com/quote/878063

Kahlil Gibran. Provocative Interaction quote. https://www.azquotes.com/quote/529713

Mark Twain. https://www.azquotes.com/quote/298610

Chris Argyris first featured 'The Ladder of Inference' in Peter Senge, *The Fifth Discipline Fieldbook The art and practice of the learning organisation.* 2006.

Eric Berne. *Games People Play: An Introduction to Transactional Analysis.* Grove Press, 1965.

Anthony Willoughby. Author, entrepreneur, explorer, team builder. Founder of 'I Will Not Complain'. In this chapter we talked about the concept of not complaining and we thought it would be interesting if you could see the origins of that and understand how we could apply this to team work when the situation demanded a focus from negativity to a more positive outlook .

Thank you to Anthony Willoughby for introducing co-author Sandy and her husband to Kenya where she worked for eleven years building schools and studying leadership with the Maasai tribes.

Phyllis Victoria Bristow. Grandmother to co-author Sandy. A leader, mentor, mother, and the best grandmother to teach lessons of life and compassion.

Rudyard Kipling. The Kipling Society. https://www.kiplingsociety.co.uk

CHAPTER 7

US Air Force. Air Force Leadership. AFP 35-49, 1985.

Marsha L Clark. *Embrace Your Power: A Woman's guide to Authentic Leadership & Meaningful Relationships*

CHAPTER 8

Gallup research on workforce engagement. https://www.gallup.com.

Lao Tzu. https://www.brainyquote.com/quotes/lao_tzu_379183

Stephen Covey. https://www.azquotes.com/quote/1350808

Colin Powell. 'General Colin Powell's Leadership Primer'. https://ung.edu/institute-leadership-strategic-studies/_uploads/files/colin-powell-leadership.pdf.

Ken Blanchard. *Whale Done: The Power of Positive Relationships.* Free Press, 2002.

Patrick Lencioni. *Teamwork: The Five Dysfunctions of a Team.* The Table Group. https://www.tablegroup.com/

Stephen M Covey. *Speed of Trust.* https://www.speedoftrust.com.

CHAPTER 9

Jack Welch. https://www.brainyquote.com/quotes/jack_welch_833427

Henry Ford. https://www.linkedin.com/pulse/two-undeniable-truths-quotes-noah-marks/

Richard Branson. CEO and founder of Virgin Group. Manages his company based on the motto https://www.azquotes.com/quote/594793.

Chan Master Fuchan Yuan. https://www.linkedin.com/pulse/essence-leadership-humility-clarity-courage-project-joey-perugino-/

Johann Wolfgang von Goethe. 1749–1832. Writer and polymath. https://www.quotes.net/quote/1201.

General George S Patton. https://www.brainyquote.com/quotes/george_s_patton_159766.

CHAPTER 10

Bill Gates. https://www.brainyquote.com/quotes/bill_gates_173262.

Yousif Asfour. Other quotes used in this chapter are partly attributed to Yousif (co-author) who has used them so often he has lost sight of the origins but knows they work in practice!

2 out of 3 Rule. Based on the principles of Agile and The Triple Constraint Theory of Project Management.

We value our working relationship that has been built on respect and trust over the years. We have worked together for almost two decades in both a client-consultant and consulting-partners capacity, sharing our experiences with many existing and would-be leaders. Although we approach things in slightly different ways, we have spent many hours, after the close of business, debating the issues we've been confronted with. We have met some challenging situations and have found being allies invaluable. But we have learned to play to our strengths, and we know that we share the goal of motivating others to build on and develop their own and their teams' strengths. We have helped develop teams into more productive, better performing teams, shifted unhelpful cultural practices to healthier environments, and helped individuals to grow and take on more leadership accountabilities.

Many of the situations we describe in the book are based on real life encounters that we resolved by connecting and engaging with the leaders we were working with. Some leaders have been in situ already and others we have developed, based on our experience or instinct, to take on a leadership role. As a CIO, Yousif has executed all the ideas in this book to earn IT the respect of the organizations he has worked in, while Sandy has supported him in the development of softer skills and leadership coaching. We both appreciate that IQ and technical skills matter, but we are also aware that emotional intelligence is a key area for all leaders to develop.

We share a love of Dr Seuss and a similar sense of humor. We both love telling stories and over the years have been able to add to these with teams sharing their own with us. We have tried to inject some fun into the book because we both know the value of laughter and encourage people to enjoy what they do.

I have had the privilege to work with some very courageous people in my career. Courageous in as much as they have been willing to take personal risks in their own development, be vulnerable and challenge themselves to stretch beyond their comfort zones to become better leaders.

I have also learned a great deal from the people I have led and coached and have been able to use that learning to help more leaders, whether starting out on their leadership journey, or looking to find more potential in themselves.

So, I'd like to extend my heartfelt thanks to the many people I have engaged with and met in the various organizations worldwide. No matter which country I have worked in, I've met people who wanted to make a positive difference in their work environments.

There have also been leaders in my career that have made a big impact on me. They trusted me, they challenged me, they gave me the space to be autonomous and accountable and I learned so much.

I was also blessed to have had a mother and grandmother who taught me the value of honesty and helped me to live the values that helped me to connect and relate to others. They both walked the talk as we often ask of our leaders. I have also often tried new ideas out on my husband and used his responses in my training, sometimes resulting in great hilarity and other times to offer examples of his leadership to reinforce what good leadership can look like. He does so many of the things we talk about in the book naturally but loves to learn new things too.

Meeting leaders like Yousif has also enabled me to be creative and try new things. I remember telling him about an untested approach I was going to try out with 16 of his leaders and as we were walking into the room, he panicked and said, 'I'm not sure this is going to work, shall we do something else?' I asked him to trust me, he did, and we had a productive session. More trust between us resulted. He still, however, finishes some conversations where I get over excited, with the 'so what' question!

We have said for years we would write a book and we have. We have had help from our editor, and our designer has been incredible and we've learned so much from them both.

My leadership journey started at a very young age, and I have many people to thank for that. Listing all of them requires writing a book on its own – something I may consider doing at some point.

The foundational core values on which everything is built were laid by my father and grandmother who, after the untimely death of my mother, raised me from an early age, and I am eternally grateful to them.

I also have my brother and cousins to thank for letting me experiment on them with leadership skills as we built villages and 'fought wars' with our neighbors in the woods during the summers.

Interestingly enough, I learned the politics of leadership in the most unlikely environments: volunteering as a scout leader, joining clubs at school and college, and teaching at Sunday School. These were great experiences and I am eternally thankful for everyone I interacted with.

Although a geek and introvert by nature, I have my wife, Brenda, to thank for giving me the courage to open up. My communication and presentation skills were further refined during my doctorate studies, and I have my advisors, Professor Gail Carpenter and Professor Stephen Grossberg to thank for that. In particular, they drove me to be clear, succinct, focus on the message, and to always write my ideas down before sharing them.

I cut my teeth in executive leadership at a startup in Boulder, Colorado. This is where I learned many key leadership skills from the founders, Art Zeile and Joel Daly, and from Dan Rojas, my neighbor, colleague and friend. My leadership skills were further refined by my mentor and coach, James Bruce, who, among many things, served as the first CIO at MIT.

I would also like to thank all the people I have worked with over the years, without whom we wouldn't have any experiences or stories to write about.

Of course, this book would not have happened without Sandy, my colleague, partner and friend whom I have worked with and learned from for almost two decades. And of course, I cannot thank enough our editor Reem Haddad, and our book designer Hani Asfour, who put up with both Sandy and I.

Thank you to everyone who has contributed to my journey and our book, whether mentioned here or not. I hope that you got out of our encounter as much as I have.

A FINAL THOUGHT

Are you familiar with the
exercise that asks
**'What do you want to be
remembered for?'**
Now, apply the question to your
leadership faculties.
**Imagine you are leaving the
team and they are gathered
to remember you.**
Which would you rather hear?

'I liked him, but I don't think I ever knew him.'
'I really liked him. He was real.'

'She never used all my skills.'
'I learned so much from her.'

'He was just waiting to work with another team.'
'He has made a big difference to this team.'

'I don't feel she treated us equally.'
'She treated us all with respect, as individuals.'

'He always had an answer for his boss.'
'He had good relationships with all levels.'

YOU GET THE IDEA.
THE CHOICE IS YOURS.